I had the opportunity to read this book before its publication and, once involved, I had difficulty putting it down. It is an amazing true story of my friends, Michael and Karen, and their most serious trial and tribulations with life-threatening medical problems. Their great faith and love of God gave them strength and carried them through to the plans that He has for their lives. They are and have been very active in service to their church and spreading Jesus Christ's love to others.

- ***John H. Van Houten,*** *Community Leader and Philanthropist*

"God has asked (encouraged, forced) Michael to share His presence (activity) in Michael's life. In this book, Michael and his wife, Karen, share his remarkable story of healing from cancer. It is a story of coming to Jesus in reluctant submission and surrender. We also learn about the origin and joy of the F.R.O.G. ministry, which continues to 'plague' Flagstaff today. I was impressed with Michael's honesty about his battles with anger and impatience which we all fight to overcome."

- ***John Mauk, MD*** *[and "Clergymate" — i.e. husband to Pastor Karol Brechiesen]*

This is one of the most moving stories I have ever read. Several things in Michael's story touched me: I am sure I cannot begin to understand the pain, the agony and, undoubtedly, the feeling of hopelessness he experienced with cancer & being too sick to cry. I will never look at a frog again without remembering what F.R.O.G. stands for - Fully Rely On God. I appreciate his comments regarding the homeless; I have walked with the homeless and found faith, hope and heart-wrenching stories, but nothing compared to the ministries of Abraham, John, Paul & Luke. Michael's comments on ushering are so 'right on' – I, too, enjoy "Serving the Lord's children while honoring Him." He is missed, more than he can ever imagine.

- ***Ken Hext,*** *retired county employee and church usher*

I met Michael during my Walk to Emmaus. During the weekend, we had a chance conversation where he shared much of his life story as it pertains to his fight with cancer … and, primarily, how God has moved in his life through nothing less than a FROG. I will remember that conversation but, even more, I will always remember the words on these pages as they speak so intimately and genuinely of the true nature of our Lord. There is every evidence that they were not written by Michael himself but, as he so eloquently phrased it, "He [God] always held the pen."

- ***Ian Salsman,*** *gr*

It doesn't take long for the reader of this book to discover that he is holding a valuable rare account of how God can and often does, heal in a miraculous way.

Especially here, the cancer sufferer can find hope by looking into this case of chronic disease.

Very soon into the book one gets the feeling that he's reading someone else's mail. It's that personally and touchingly written. It reaches past the usual and goes deep into one's sympathy and understanding for the cancer patient.

Most of all, the book is not ashamed to tell it all – the good, the bad and the ugly – how the long-time cancer patient feels and thinks. It goes way past traditional and conventional medical approaches, venturing into seemingly unchartered personal spiritual discovery. Michael shares things I've never heard before – observations on dealing with severe illness in a very deep way.

I was struck right away with the impression that while all the medical procedures were being tried and applied to treating cancer, family support was so very crucial. Karen's helpfulness was absolutely essential to Michael's recovery. Sacrifice after sacrifice was made so that Michael could win the battle.

The insights Michael shares from his spiritual journey are remarkable. [How] he goes from what some folks would characterize as a nominal Christian faith to a daily, yea, even a moment by moment "living" faith in God is very instructive.

It was for me. My faith through hard times has been strengthened and further secured.

No wonder then, that I have a little green frog sitting in one of the most trafficked places in my home – to remind me always to "Fully Rely On God"!

> *- **Glen E. Allen**, Founding Executive Director*
> *FaithWorks – Christians in Mission, Flagstaff, Arizona*

"Michael Bradford has written a gripping account of his battle with cancer and faith. His book takes us through his journey of challenges and opportunities where he comes to the realization that he has no choice but to "Fully Rely on God". Most of us have been touched by cancer in someone very close to us. His book will help you to better understand why cancer is often characterized as a "battle or fight" and give you hope and courage for the days ahead."

> *- **Rich Payne**, neighbor*

Fully Rely On God!

In His Arms

My Weakness His Strength

Written by God. Penned by

Michael and Karen Bradford

DEDICATION

For my Lord God who created me.
For His Son Christ Jesus who saved me.
For the Holy Spirit (the Comforter) who is my guide.
For seven ministering angels that watch over me.
For my wife and best friend, Karen, and all those who prayed with and over me, may God bless you everyone.

ACKNOWLEDGEMENTS

After I had completed the manuscript for this book, I wondered, "What now?" I knew I was finished with what I had been asked to write and Karen, my wife, was busy editing, checking chronology and generally massaging the text. However, I knew God had instructed me to write my story in order to share it with others, to give hope and courage to those who were struggling with the monster I had battled.

At first, we printed copies of the manuscript and gave them to friends, family and church members. The book was passed around and I heard from many that they and/or family had been inspired by what they read. Although home printed copies were good, we knew what was really needed was to have the book published to be able to get it to a broader audience.

People would tell us they had a friend/sister/acquaintance who was/or worked with an editor or a publisher. But time and again we were told that these people were too busy to even look at what I had written. In frustration, I asked God why He chose me to write this book. He told me, "I chose a child to tell My story." As I prayed over what should be my next steps, He sent other children to help this child.

Many people gave us encouragement and prayers – too many to list individually. However, I must thank Rich Rice. After reading the manuscript, he said it was a powerful story but it needed something to tie everything together. The result was the Epilogue.

But this book wouldn't even be in your hands if it weren't for Ian and Carol Salsman. Just when I was beginning to wonder if I would ever see this book in print, Ian and Carol approached me at a gathering of Emmaus pilgrims and said they wanted to help get the book published. They said they felt that God wanted them to help us. Ian told us he is a graphic designer and he wanted to design the cover of the book. He also told us about Snowfall Press and said he could help us navigate their website to prepare the book for printing. Ian is responsible for the the sleek interior layout. Carol lent a proofreader's eye to root out the various and sundry errors we had missed. Ian and Carol have worked so hard to bring this to fruition that I don't have words to thank them. So I thank God for them every day.

And then there's my wife......

TABLE OF CONTENTS

PART 1

UNDER THE SHADOW 1

WALK TO EMMAUS 27

TIME CAPSULE 36

IRREDEEMABLE ABYSS 41

FATHER, SON & HOLY SPIRIT 44

IRREDEEMABLE ABYSS 2 46

MIRACLES 49

WEIRD OF HEARING 53

CLIMBING HIGHER 56

PART 2

DIVINE APPOINTMENTS 71

    Battle Dress! *76*

    Temptation *78*

    Fear of Death *88*

    Impatience *96*

    Patience *100*

    Lee Ann Le Picard *103*

    Mankind *126*

PART 3

COMPULSION TO WRITE 145

TITUS 146

KISMET 149

USHERS 153

ANGELA 155

WALKING WITH THE HOMELESS . . . 159

RED, WHITE AND BLUE 171

PART 4

SPIRITUAL MODALITY 179

MUSINGS 186

EPILOGUE 199

PREFACE

At the beginning of 2005, I was pretty content with my life. My marriage was good; my finances were stable; the kids were grown with kids of their own – not too much stress, no need to question what life meant. I was muddling along in my lukewarm faith and my Sunday go-to-meeting Christianity, wrapped up in the small burdens of everyday life. But then in my fifty-seventh year something happened to me that changed everything. I was diagnosed with cancer.

During the life-and-death struggle that ensued, I discovered the true power of prayer, embraced the faith I had merely dabbled with before, and developed a real relationship with God. I had experiences that were nothing short of miraculous. Beyond the miracles of healing, I had encounters that went beyond mere coincidence. In a string of divine appointments, I met people who encouraged me or were encouraged by me.

Even in the midst of the struggle, I felt an inner prompting to tell my story. If I ignored the prompting, it became a strong urging and, if further ignored, an irresistible impulse. I have told parts of my story to many people – family, friends, and strangers. If anyone would listen, I would blurt out the amazing things that happened to me. Occasionally someone would say, "That's a powerful story. You should write a book." My response was, "Yeah, maybe."

But God wasn't satisfied with, "Yeah, maybe." Slowly I began to feel the Holy Spirit nudging me to put this story on paper. But I was stubborn, so the nudging, prompting and urging began again. I finally accepted the fact that this was a direct order. God wanted me to write my story. Now, I'm not a writer. Oh, sure, I can write but I'm not "A Writer." There had to be some mistake, but God doesn't make mistakes and when He tells you to write something, you write it.

At first I thought I could convince my wife, Karen, to write this book for me. After all, she never left my side during the treatments, doctor appointments, and surgical procedures. She knew about the miracles of healing with which I had been blessed. She was with me when I met most of the wonderful people who brought me messages of hope and encouragement. Karen is a skillful writer with an extensive vocabulary. She's a walking-talking thesaurus, for crying out loud.

Although Karen and I are kindred spirits, in the end I knew who was going to put this story to word. I knew the story had to be told. But why in heaven's name did He pick me to be a ghost-writer for the Holy Ghost? I'm not a saint. I'm just an ordinary, sinful man. By the way, did I mention, I'm not "A Writer"? I understood that this was a deeply personal story and the thought of writing it put me way outside my comfort zone. However, I was the one who actually walked through this valley. Only I could express the fear and the pain, the hope and the comfort I experienced. I realized later that God would use my personal insight to benefit some other souls and bring them His hope and comfort during their time of distress.

In a fit of defiance, I sat on the sofa with a blank tablet on my lap and a pen in my hand.

"Fine," I thought. "Lord, if you want me to write this book, you'd better be holding the pen."

In the back of my mind, I could hear Him say, "I've always held the pen!"

When I acquiesced to His will, God placed his hand on my shoulder, whispered in my ear, and kindled a flame in my heart. That certainly didn't mean it was easy. At times the process of writing this book seemed nearly as difficult as the physical struggle I endured just to be alive to write it. There were plenty of times when I was ready to give up and delete my file. But this message is much too powerful and too spiritual to be cast aside.

It was especially difficult for me to write about the pain and suffering and fear I experienced during my treatment and recovery. I would just as soon forget it all. In some cases, I prayed over every single word just to get through. But the hard parts of the story are essential to appreciating the joy and the blessings that make up the good outcomes.

I'm grateful that the Holy Spirit, The Comforter, urged me to write my story because I will feel doubly blessed if just one other person is encouraged by my experience. Besides, every minute I've spent writing, reading, and working on this book refreshes my memories of the blessings I've received during this trial.

There were so many blessings bestowed upon me and my family. I've experienced more kindness, compassion, and goodwill in the past three years than all my previous years of life.

Before cancer, I was always looking for someone or something to complain about or blame, rather than someone or something to be thankful for. I was counting my blessings on one hand while using a calculator with the other to curse life negatively.

It was not until I was faced with my own mortality that I realized how to live life to its fullest. Now I understand that loving what you do is more important than doing what you love. Cancer saved my spiritual life and, like most life-threatening diseases, it led to a cure for sinning.

As children of the Lord, we are instructed to pray for one another. When I became ill, churches, families and individuals around the world lifted me up in prayer. I know God answers prayers. Despite my sinfulness, He must have thought, "OK. I hear you. I'll take another look at my child."

I hope to honor Him with this book by writing about the things I was allowed to see and experience. Some of those experiences are so powerful and compelling, that when I read them, I am still stirred spiritually and emotionally because I know, "It's not about me."

I pray that the words in this book will send 10,000 to flight and will bring praise and honor to our Lord Jesus. Amen.

PART 1

UNDER THE SHADOW

UNDER THE SHADOW

It was five months from diagnosis through treatment, then back to work. This is how the Holy Spirit found me, his lost lamb. I pray that the reader will persevere through the painful stages to find the glorious rewards of that perseverance, just as I did.

THE STORM CLOUDS GATHER

My wife, Karen, was working for a major insurance company in Pensacola, Florida, after hurricane Ivan had wreaked havoc on its way through. She went there just before Thanksgiving but was home for a short break over Christmas.

"Why don't you drive over after New Year's? Some of our volunteers have to go home soon. Steve says he'll need to replace them and he would really be glad to have someone with your experience ready to step in when they depart." Karen then added, "Maybe you could check with the doctor."

She knew I'd been to the doctor shortly after she left town. After two months of self-medicating with over-the-counter treatments, I still had a pesky sore throat. The doctor put me on the "purple pill" for heartburn, thinking I might be developing Barrett's esophagus. After another month, the pills weren't working.

Karen flew back to Pensacola and I went back to my doctor. Peering down my throat he said, "Looks like you've got a lot of drainage from your sinuses. That can cause major throat irritation. I'll give you a prescription for some nose drops that should clear it up for you. I don't see any reason why you can't drive to Pensacola."

Karen's job takes her out of town frequently and for long periods of time. But we've been blessed that I've been able to pick up temp jobs with her company. The hours are brutal, but at least we can be together, and we work with a good group of people.

As I jumped in my car and headed down the highway, I thought, "I can't wait to get back to work so I can be with my wife."

I made the drive from Flagstaff to Pensacola in two days. It had been three and a half months since Ivan hit the coast, but some of the street signs were still missing. Heck, I would have missed my exit off I-10 if the sign hadn't been propped up against a pine tree.

I called Karen on her cell and met her at the temporary office, which was set up in a roller rink named Dreamland. It was a strange arrangement, but office space for 150 people was hard to come by after a disaster like Hurricane Ivan. Together we drove off to her temporary apartment, which was in a retirement home. Living quarters for all the out-of-town workers were also in short supply. The position I came for hadn't opened up yet, so I settled in to rest after my hectic trip.

There wasn't much happening in the retirement home, but it was definitely quiet. That was good because I really did need rest. I wasn't feeling any better than when I left Flagstaff. In fact, I was feeling worse. Although I used them as directed, the nose drops weren't helping. Boy, my throat really hurt. I needed to feel better before I started to work.

I called Karen. "Hi, honey. Is there a clinic anywhere in town that is seeing patients? There's no phone book in this place."

She checked with some of the locals and called me back. "There's a walk-in clinic between the office and the apartment. Several people from the office have gone there but they say there's sometimes a long wait."

She gave me the number and address, then I called to get their hours. I vowed to myself I'd make it a point to "walk in" as soon as they opened.

I was first in line the next morning. They swabbed my throat for cultures and gave me antibiotics. "We'll call you when we get the results."

The clinic called about a week later to say I had strep. Okay, I could deal with that but I wished the antibiotics would kick in. I'd be starting work on Monday, so I made another run by the clinic. Another round of antibiotics. "Must be stubborn stuff," I thought.

Finally! I had arrived at Dreamland. It's always weird to arrive at a new "catastrophe" office, but this was the first time I'd seen one set up in a roller rink. This one was a huge peach-colored metal building. The name "Dreamland" was painted across the front in the center of a mural which showed the sun setting behind palm trees, tropical flowers and a parrot. Oh, and a wild looking dude on roller skates was blasting through the scenery.

Inside it was a pretty typical set up. Lots of folding tables had been arranged as desks with phones and internet lines for the laptops. Tables with PCs were arranged in the far back of the huge open space. That was where I'd be working. What wasn't typical were the highly polished floor – pale aqua, almost like ice – and the royal purple carpeting that covered the lower half of the walls. Above the carpeting, the peach-colored wall was decorated with airbrush fantasies of skaters and the Blue Angels. Hey, it's Pensacola. But the most unusual sight was the huge mirrored disco ball that hung in the middle of it all.

"Hey, Michael's here!"

"Hi, Michael!"

Karen began introducing me to the inmates of my new asylum. I already knew many of them since we'd worked together before. The coordinator of the operation…second in command to Steve – was a pleasant man named Hal. His mild professional manner hid the fact that Hal had a wild side. Hal grew up in Pensacola and worked at the skating rink in his youth.

As I would find out later, he occasionally made general announcements from the DJ booth. He'd even been known to turn on the music, complete with spot lights and disco ball then skate around the floor and between the desks. He gave the disco ball another workout when he brought in an Elvis impersonator for Steve's birthday. Hal's management style was what we needed during those long difficult work days. Sure, we would be working hard, but we would laugh and have a little fun to keep our spirits up.

I was glad to be back at work. But a lot of folks seemed to have coughs, colds, upper respiratory problems. Karen developed bronchitis so bad the walk-in clinic gave her inhalation therapy on top of the antibiotics. The building we were in suffered considerable roof damage in the storm, and rain continued to enter despite the many tarps on the roof.

"Maybe that's why I can't get over this thing," I thought. "Maybe there's mold in the insulation. I know there are dust and other irritants in the air."

Well, the doctors at the clinic finally decided I needed to see an ear, nose and throat specialist.

"I need to find an ENT doctor. Anyone have any ideas?" I asked the group.

One of my coworkers replied, "I've been seeing a real good one. I'll get you his name and number."

Encouraged by the vote of confidence, I made an appointment with Dr. Bly. After taking a history, he put a scope through my nose down to my voice box. "Well, you don't have cancer!" he exclaimed and smiled reassuringly. "I'm going to order several tests to rule out what can kill you."

I was glad to hear there was no cancer. But despite Dr. Bly's optimistic pronouncements, I felt an ominous foreboding echo in my mind, "I think there's something seriously wrong with me."

I was sent to have blood drawn at the Urgent Care Facility of the Pensacola Regional Medical Center. I was alone in the waiting area when an emaciated young man in his late twenties joined me. His eyes were haggard and cavernous. His belt was marked by a half dozen extra holes which had been punched in the leather to secure the belt and buckle to his bony frame. The extra leather protruding beyond the buckle was twisted and wrapped several times around his belt. As I gazed at this gaunt specter, I could tell he was at death's door.

I was there for a simple blood test, part of the "rule out what can kill you" regimen. I was the only person in the waiting room. Plenty of space, but this man walked to the chair directly opposite me and sat. While I stared at this harbinger of things to come, he spoke.

"My name is Jeremy. You know, that's a form of Jeremiah."

"I'm Michael, like the archangel," I replied. "I'm here for a blood test. The doctor can't figure out what's wrong with me."

"I'm here for a blood test too," he said softly. "But I already know what's wrong with me. I have cancer. It's terminal. I'm here to see if I have enough white blood cells left to allow me to keep on working. I've only got weeks but if I can keep on working… Well, that's more money for the family."

I looked at the wedding band on Jeremy's hand and wondered, "Will he die with the faith and courage I have yet to muster in my fifty-seven years of living?" I have always clung to the belief that death is not the final failure in life, but rather a rest marking one's accomplishments at life's end. A nice thought, but what did this man who's half my age accomplish in what little life he was given?

I felt awkward trying to converse with a dying man I didn't know. But I was drawn to Jeremy. Some might call it morbid curiosity, but I wanted to know what held this man together in the face of hopelessness.

"I really didn't want to do it. You know…the cancer treatments," he said looking at his hands. "It's only giving me a few extra weeks, maybe months. But my wife begged me."

Then Jeremy's face lit up as he told me about his wife and four year old daughter, speaking of them as if they were a family with hopes and dreams for the future.

While I was crying and screaming on the inside for the Lord to have mercy and grant this man more time, Jeremy smiled at me and said, "Every day is a gift from the Lord. I know that my life is not my own and it's not for me to direct the path my life will take."

Later when I was writing about this incident, I was drawn to the book of Jeremiah where I found this passage: *"I know, O LORD, that a man's life is not his own; it is not for man to direct his steps." Jeremiah 10:23 (New International Version)* These were the very words Jeremy had spoken to me that day.

Although I didn't know it as I sat chatting with this young man, I was suffering from the early effects of a rare and often fatal form of throat cancer. Looking back now, I know that the Lord sent Jeremy to that waiting room to prepare me for what was to come.

Jeremy spoke to me of God's promise saying, "The Lord is with me and I am with him."

It was as if a window to Jeremy's soul was opened. The light of his spirit flowed over me and his words comforted me. When I close my eyes, I can still see that frail shell of a man imbued with the power of the Holy Spirit. I firmly believe God sent an angel to guide me to where He wanted me to be.

"He makes the winds His messengers, Flaming fire His ministers." Psalm 104:4.

For some the prospect of dying is intimidating, for death not only separates us from our loved ones, but it thrusts us from this earth into the unknown. I will smile in the face of death for my consciousness will not be thrust into the unknown but be lifted up on wings of angels. If it pleases my Father, I pray that I, like Jeremy, can be a messenger for the Holy Spirit.

Karen was waiting for me in the car when I reached the parking garage. "What took so long?" she asked. "I would have gone in with you, but you said it was a quick blood drawing."

"It was supposed to be. I don't know what the holdup was but I met a very interesting man," I replied. Then I told her about Jeremy.

"If I had been there, you might not have spoken with him. Maybe you were meant to be the only two in that waiting room," she mused. Looking back, I'm positive she was right.

After the tests came back, I returned to see Dr. Bly. "Well, the tests were negative," he reported. "We'll have to do some more tests."

Back at the apartment, I told Karen about the results. I had been hoping for answers and had none. Frustrated, I slammed the latest antibiotic prescription on the counter and blurted out, "I bet I have cancer. They just can't figure it out."

"Don't talk like that," she retorted, obviously upset at my outburst. "The doctor says you don't!" Her own frustration was evident in her voice.

I underwent the additional tests the doctor had ordered. After the second battery of tests proved negative, Dr. Bly didn't sound so confident, "Something's killing you and I don't know what it is." He ordered more tests.

I told Karen what the doctor said. "He said something's killing me. I told you! It's cancer and they won't find it until they perform the autopsy." She just put her arms around me. What could she say?

I had arrived in January but then March came. I could tell it would not be long before spring engulfed Pensacola. Over the weeks of work, doctor visits and tests, my condition had continued to deteriorate. Karen and my coworkers could see how weak I had become. I really wanted to go home.

Finally in the middle of March, Karen announced jubilantly, "We have a release date! We're out of here next week!" That was one thing I loved about our work: we were excited when we arrived and even happier when we left.

It was with enormous relief that I called Dr. Bly to let him know I was leaving and would be returning to Flagstaff. He requested that I come see him the day before I left. Sure, why not?

When I stopped at his office, I didn't have to wait long. Dr. Bly saw me right away. He handed me a copy of my medical records and said bluntly, "You're dying and I don't know why. You need to go see a doctor as soon as you get home."

I was too shocked to say anything. I may have mumbled, "Thanks" or "Good-bye." As I took my file and left, I wondered to myself, "Go see a doctor? I thought I just did." I walked to my car with my head down, never looking up.

Now more than ever, we were anxious to get back to Flagstaff. We had friends who were doctors or knew doctors. We longed for our confidants who would be able to tell us who was the best in town.

Unfortunately the trip, home that should have taken three days tops took us seven days. We had to detour through Denver for Karen to attend a conference. While Karen anxiously sat through two and a half days of meetings, I sat in our hotel room unable to do much more than stare at the ceiling. I was physically weak and emotionally drained. The evening before we left, our son Eric called to tell us one of our cats had died. Poor, old Raistlin. We'd had him for sixteen years, but I couldn't even cry at his passing. I could only watch the miles pass by as Karen wept off and on during the last leg of the trip.

We arrived home totally exhausted. Karen made some calls to friends for a name and I called for an appointment with the recommended ENT specialist. Fortunately, he could see me in one week which is actually very quick for Flagstaff. Then, moving like zombies, we went about the tasks of washing and putting away clothes, sorting a couple of months of mail, and assessing the housekeeping we'd need to accomplish after our absence.

On the day of my appointment Karen was working on one of the many projects on our "to do" list, so I drove over to the doctor's office alone. I filled out the requisite paperwork and handed over my file from Dr. Bly then took a seat in the waiting room. Before I had time to select a magazine, the nurse called my name and escorted me to a brightly lit examination room. Once I was seated in the exam chair, she placed my folder in a file rack and closed the door as she exited.

I glanced around the room at the now-familiar tools of the ENT trade. I'd had most of them poked into my head by this time. Just seeing the laryngoscope made me gag. On the wall hung the standard chart of the human head and neck, the nasal and oral cavities colorfully illustrated along with the esophagus and larynx. I could see the path the pain took down my throat. A tap at the door interrupted my reverie and a tall man entered while perusing my file. Dr. Bowens gave me a firm handshake and asked me what was going on.

"I've had a sore throat for months. Dr. Fisher gave me Nexium and some nose drops. Then I went to work in Pensacola for a while. The clinic there put me on antibiotics. That didn't help so I went to an ENT - Dr. Bly…who ran all kinds of tests on me. He couldn't figure out what was wrong." I chuckled, "He told me to see a doctor when I got home, so here I am."

Dr. Bowens smiled. "Okay, then. Let's have a look." He picked up a tongue depressor and I said, "Aahhh." After pressing down my tongue, he peered at my throat with his lamp. His brow knitted, he drew back from me, looked down at the floor, and walked over to the wall chart. He lifted his hand to point at the illustrated throat but dropped his arm back to his side. He turned and came back to where I sat. Then this man I had just met wrapped his arms around me, and whispered, "I'm so sorry. You have cancer."

After a moment, Dr. Bowens told me he would set an appointment for a biopsy the next morning and stepped out of the room. I sat in the chair, numb from the news, my mind shouting, "Oh, dear God!!! Now what?" I could hear Dr. Bowens on the phone down the hall. He spoke to my now ex-personal physician Dr. Fisher and then Dr. Bly in Florida. I heard him tell one and then the other quite forcefully, "YOU MISSED IT, YOU JUST PLAIN MISSED IT!!!"

I stood up, left the doctor's office, got in my car and drove home in a daze. When I got back home, Karen and my son Eric were standing in the dining room chatting when I walked in. They turned toward me and Karen asked, "How'd it go, sweetie? Did the doctor figure out what's wrong?"

Still in shock I blurted out, "I have cancer." My wife and son both stood there with their mouths open, staring at me.

The following morning Dr. Bowens performed the biopsy in surgery. The results came back positive. I had squamous cell carcinoma of the post pharyngeal wall. I was referred to an oncologist and there was a flurry of activity: PET scan, bone scan, X-ray, MRI, CT scan, and a meeting with a social worker. And then – wait for a month. "Wait for a month?" I kept asking, "Why? Let's get started. I've already wasted months. Let's kill this thing!"

The answer was that they were going to use a fairly new technique that would more specifically target the cancer and do less damage to the normal tissue. All of the data from all of the tests was being processed by computer. The results would guide the IMRT (Intensity Modulation Radiation Treatment) machine during my treatments. That was what was taking so long.

In hindsight, that extra time turned out to be God's blessing, and God's timing is always perfect. I was already under my optimum weight from the months of feeling so poorly and Karen knew how the treatments were going to affect me. She managed to pack forty pounds on me in four weeks. It was a good thing she did. I lost fifty pounds during the treatment.

In addition to the physical fortification I received during that interminable wait, I began a spiritual and emotional fortification. By phone and e-mail, the call went out to believers near and far. Pastor Karol brought prayer warriors to pray over me. My church family gathered around me with prayers and promises of more prayers to come, building up a framework of faith to support me.

Neighbor Richard Payne came to my home and told me stories from the Bible. Rich had such a wonderfully straight-forward, child-like way of telling these stories. I really looked forward to his visits because we became like children talking, praying and playing. One of the stories in particular included that of Lazarus recounted in John 11. As Rich told me the story how Jesus was deeply moved by the death of His friend and He called out to him, "Lazarus, come out." Rich paused dramatically. "You knew he wasn't really going to stay dead, didn't you?" he said, smiling, boyishly.

All of this was occurring during Lent and the build up to Easter always brings a proliferation of stuffed animals to local stores. I was pretty down – okay, majorly depressed…so Karen had picked up a stuffed frog for me while she was grocery shopping. She knew that I've always liked frogs and hoped this would cheer me up. Man, this one was a doozy – bright lime green, head the size of a soccer ball, and a smile that went from ear to ear. Looking at that smile I had to smile back.

The frog took up residence on the dining room table so he could look through the foyer to the front door. The next time Pastor Karol came by the house to pray, she couldn't miss the huge frog with arms spread wide in greeting. When she saw it, she said, "F.R.O.G. – Fully Rely On God." I'd never heard that before. Little did I know how that phrase would change my life.

While the waiting was still almost unbearable, the frog on the table became a "presence." He was too big and too bright to be ignored. When anyone came to visit, I told them the FROG acronym. And every time I saw him, I thought, "Fully Rely On

God. Fully Rely On God." It became my mantra. I told Karen, "I'm going to take that frog with me to all of my treatments."

"Good," she said. "He'll remind both of us to Fully Rely On God." Finally the call came from the cancer center. I needed some pre-treatment work done and counseling completed before they could begin the radiation. I walked through the clinic door with my wife at my side and my big stuffed frog in my arms. The frog was an instant hit with the reception team. But the first thing everyone asked is, "What's his name?" Until then he had just been "the frog," but I figured I'd have to come up with a name. It didn't take long. That very day the radiation techs suggested "Rad." They told me that everything that comes into the unit is stamped RAD – short for radiation. The word "rad" has also been used recently by some past teenage generation as a shortened form of the slang term "radical" and it really seemed to fit. I like it! He officially became Rad.

INTO THE VALLEY

I was lying on a table at the cancer treatment center. Karen and Rad were sitting in the corner. The oncologist and two nurses placed a large, wet, hot mesh netting material over my face, pushing and shaping the material around my face and upper torso almost to my waist. With towels, they patted the excess moisture from the net until it began to shrink and harden. After the mold cooled, they removed it and placed it on a metal frame. Boy, it was good to get that thing off me! I couldn't breathe through my nose and I couldn't see either.

Next, I was taken to another room and placed on an MRI table. The mask, which was now dry and had shrunk considerably, was placed over my face and body from my waist up and bolted down to the table I was laying on. Normally I am not claustrophobic, but I was getting that way real fast. In desperation I begged, "Can you please cut holes for my eyes?" They removed the mask, cut holes for the eyes and bolted it back in place. Then I was left alone in the chamber for what seemed like years but was more like thirty minutes. I was breathing through my teeth and so frantic I couldn't concentrate on prayers. All I wanted to do was to turn this machine over and escape. As the screening progressed, I was screaming inside and that scream wasn't far from coming out of my mouth like some deranged demon. When the test was complete, they marked the mask in various places where the cancer had been detected. Finally, I was released from this torturous hell.

Next I saw the oncologist. He explained to me that I would have to wear the mask for up to thirty minutes a day for forty treatments. It was designed to fix my position on the treatment table and keep me immobile while the machine did its precision work. I balked. "Nope! I can't do it. You'll have to knock me out or something. I wouldn't wear that if my life depended on it."

The doctor replied, "You will and it does. Your cancer is so close to the spinal column that it is inoperable."

A flurry of thoughts raced through my mind. "What do you mean, 'your cancer'…it's not my cancer; I don't claim it for myself. And I am not claustrophobic. Heck, I like to go spelunking in dark wet caves, but this? I can't! No, I won't!"

It was obvious we had to do something. So another appointment was set with the clinic social worker and…I'd soon find out… hypnotist. I remembered that when I was in the eleventh grade, one of my teachers attempted to hypnotize me in front of the class. It didn't work. But back then I was being a snotty teenager. At this juncture, my life depended on it.

Before I knew it, I was sitting in front of Sandy, hypnotist/social worker, counting backwards from ten. My wife, Karen, was in the room but I wasn't aware of her presence. When I was fully under, Sandy asked, "How do you feel…are you relaxed?"

I responded, "Frog."

Sandy looked at Karen, "What does he mean by 'frog'?"

"F.R.O.G. – Fully Rely On God," she responded. "Something our pastor told us."

"Oh."

Searching for the reason I was so terrified of wearing the mask, Sandy told me to go back through my life and look for another event that caused the same reaction. I recalled the recent biopsy of my throat. She told me to go there, and I responded vehemently, "NO!!!"

Sandy said gently, "You don't have to actually be there. Be above your body…not experiencing, just observing. Look down at the scene and tell me what you see."

"I see myself. I'm lying on a table. Dr. Bowens and two nurses are standing over me."

"Anything else?"

"I see angels."

"Angels? How many?"

"Seven. They're standing in the shape of a horseshoe around the head of the table." Suddenly I became agitated. "Something's wrong!"

"What is it? What's happening?"

"I'm having trouble breathing. Hands in my face! Tubes down my throat! I'm thrashing around, throwing the doctor and nurses about…I can't breathe…I can't breathe!!"

Sandy quickly pulled me out the trance. She had the answer. Before the biopsy the doctor gave me a shot that was supposed to make me forget the procedure but keep me somewhat lucid. But in one out of every five thousand cases the shot doesn't work. I was aware of the entire procedure on a subconscious level. No wonder I had been so sore the day after. I tore the muscles in my calves and shoulders in an attempt to escape. Now that they had the answer we would work on some relaxation techniques, and maybe they can somehow get me in the mask.

"Boy," I was thinking. "This will take a lot of F.R.O.G." I asked Karen, "How am I going to get through forty days of this?"

Then Karen reminded me, "How do you eat an elephant? One bite at a time."

RAD STAYS THE COURSE

The first day of treatment came and I arrived at the cancer center with Karen and Rad. Jan, one of the receptionists, was very excited to introduce Rad to Inky, her floppy stuffed kitty. She confided to us with childlike enthusiasm, "Tomorrow is Cinco de Mayo. Inky will be dressed up in her fancy fiesta dress for the occasion."

After exchanging pleasantries with Jan, we took a seat in the waiting room. Shortly, a dear friend and brother in Christ joined us. Norm prayed with us before I went back to the treatment room. Then he waited with Karen until I returned and we would pray again and chat afterwards. This became our routine for thirty-seven treatments. Occasionally other friends would join us at the center. But Norm was always there, with the exception of two days when he was ill. Even then it was concern for the patients at the clinic and not his own discomfort that kept Norm away.

On our way home that first day, Karen and I discussed our new acquaintance.

"Jan's such a cheerful person and the Cancer Center seems like such a sad place. She's perfect for the receptionist position there. Your mood gets a lift just talking to her."

"Yeah, and she sure is excited about dressing Inky up for Cinco de Mayo."

"Maybe we could find a costume for Rad."

"That would be fun."

So Karen fashioned a serape from a colorful dish towel. That, combined with a straw sombrero, completed Rad's fiesta look. When he arrived at the clinic the next day, Inky was suitably impressed. Seeing Rad in his outfit elicited smiles from most of the denizens of the waiting room. Granted, they were often small ones, but they were smiles nonetheless.

"Having Rad all dressed up seemed to lighten the mood for some of the folks today," I mused as we drove home.

"Well, Cinco de Mayo is over." Karen grinned at me, "Pull into the thrift shop at the bottom of the hill. Maybe we can find some other things to dress him in."

At the thrift store, just like parents of toddlers, we learned that size is no indication of fit. However, we found a few shirts and shorts sized 6-months to 2-toddler that fit his pudgy frame. His short little arms and legs meant no long sleeves or long pants. But we put together a few outfits with summer themes like beach, baseball, and even a pair of striped coveralls that gave him the appearance of a bug-eyed Casey Jones. My all time favorite, though, was a little green scrub shirt with a caduceus on the breast pocket and "doctor in training" printed across the back.

So Rad had a new outfit every few days and all of the staff knew his name. It was during these early clinic visits that we discovered Rad's special talent. He proved to be a wonderful icebreaker. His smile was disarming and invited conversation. In an atmosphere of pain and uncertainty, people will talk to a stuffed frog before they will talk to another human being. Nearly every day, Rad opened the door for me to tell someone about FROG. My faith was what was getting me through this terrible time. I would tell the story a thousand times over if it could possibly help one fellow sufferer.

As it turned out, Rad was also very good with children. While Norm and Karen waited in the lobby, I sat in the patients' waiting room until I was called into the treatment area. This was primarily a staging area and too small to accommodate many people, so relatives/friends were asked to wait in the lobby if possible. On one occasion, an older Navajo gentleman was waiting for the doctor. With him were his son, who acted as translator, and his grandson, about three years old, who was too young to be in school. I overheard their arrangements with the receptionist to keep an eye on the boy while his father escorted the patient to the back. As he sat patiently sucking on a lollipop, the boy eyed Rad thoughtfully with eyes as round as the frog's. His father leaned forward and said in a stage whisper, "I think my boy likes your friend."

The grandfather was called at the same time I was. As we three adults stood to exit, the little boy's eyes grew even wider as he stared at Rad. He never removed the lollipop from his pursed lips, but I could tell by his knitted brow that he didn't want the frog to leave. I stepped over to where the boy sat and bent over to ask him, "Can you take care of my frog while I'm gone? I think he wants to stay here with you."

Without a word, the child straightened his back and reached out for the stuffed amphibian. His round eyes gazed rapturously at Rad's face as he drew him into a snug embrace and settled back into the chair. I didn't mind leaving Rad behind; I knew he was in good hands.

After my treatment, I stopped at the reception window to find Rad waiting for me. He was still smiling his goofy smile with bits of lollipop stuck to his fuzzy green lips, remnants of a friendship offering from his keeper.

Several weeks later my friend Norm met with Karen and me at the usual time and place. We prayed together before I headed to the back for treatment and Norman stayed with Karen to wait for me. Our post treatment chats became less frequent as the radiation sessions progressed since I needed to make a hasty retreat to the house in preparation for the waves of nausea that would soon follow. Norman and Karen headed for the door with me in tow. But that day, on the sofa nearest the door, a woman sat curled up and weeping. A florescent green and yellow afghan in the bag next to her told me she was probably there for chemo treatments.

Seeing her distress in her posture, Norm and Karen stopped to comfort her. Unable to hold back the tears, she told us her name was Lisa. She was there for her first chemo treatment against breast cancer. After we had exchanged introductions, I told her, "My frog thinks your afghan is very beautiful. Great colors!"

Looking up at me and Rad while still fighting back tears Lisa said, "A friend of mine gave me a teddy bear to bring with me."

Knowing she was alone and scared, I asked her, "So where's your bear? Didn't you bring it with you?"

"No," she replied still sobbing. "How would it look for a fifty-year-old woman to be carrying a teddy bear around?"

I shoved Rad under my left arm. "How about a fifty-seven-year-old man with a FROG," I replied with a grin.

With that, she returned a shy smile and we exchanged farewells and promises to pray for each other.

Chemo Duck

A few weeks later, as I arrived at the cancer center, I saw Lisa coming from the chemo room in the back carrying her teddy bear. When she saw Rad and me, she rushed towards us. We threw our arms around each other, both of us crying and laughing as we exchanged our cuddly mascots of comfort and security. Lisa's bear wore a big button that proclaimed, "Cancer Sucks."

"Meet Berry the Bear," she said with maternal pride. "She's a regular now." Then in a conspiratorial tone she confided, "There's another lady in the back who has a stuffed duck in her overnight bag she brings with her to the treatments. But the duck is usually confined to the bag."

"Hmm, that's very interesting," I responded. "Thanks for introducing me to Berry. That's a good-looking bear you've got. I'm glad she's coming here with you." As I waved goodbye to Lisa, Rad and I turned and headed for the chemo room.

I surveyed the room which I had visited before. There were over a half dozen of God's children undergoing treatment. Each one sat in a recliner with an IV stand next to it. Most were draped with a blanket or afghan. Some were reading. Some dozed. But I knew immediately who was hiding Chemo Duck by the way she was eyeing my frog.

As I approached her, she immediately asked, "Could I hold your frog for a while?"

"Sure," I responded, "his name's Rad, short for radiation. But in return I want to see Chemo Duck."

Without the slightest hesitation, she lifted up her bag, unzipped it, and retrieved Chemo Duck holding him out in exchange for Rad. There we were, two adults growing younger by the minute in the comfort of our childish companions. Chemo Duck was out of the bag for good. And it wasn't long before others began bringing a little bit of the security from their youth.

Most, if not all, of the children undergoing cancer treatments arrive at the clinic with their favorite doll or stuffed animal to comfort them in a rather cold and inhospitable environment. Now the adults started to bring their favorite stuffed animals to console them during chemo and radiation therapy. Perhaps the doctors and staff noticed the dissimilarity between adults that carried teddy bears as opposed to books or magazines. It appeared to me that the teddy bear toting adults had a more positive outlook and responded better to the severe side effects of chemo. During one of my later visits to the center a staff member told me that volunteers were making patchwork teddy bears to give to any patient who wanted one, regardless of age.

I never told anyone at the center, but as a child I had a stuffed chimpanzee, Angel, that I carried around with me. He had a grin just about as big as Rad's. Whenever Angel was with me, I felt protected and loved. Now I know that I am surrounded by angels, both those in human form and the invisible beings that I was able to see only under hypnosis. And yes, I am protected and loved.

ROBERT

Robert appeared to be a very private man. He kept pretty much to himself as he waited for his treatment at the Cancer Center. Somewhat obsessive compulsive by nature, he couldn't stand clutter and was constantly organizing the magazines and other periodicals on the book shelves and tables. His appointment was always ahead of mine so I became familiar with his daily routine. Bob had no propensity for small talk but muttered under his breath about the reading material being outdated. In one rare overt statement he told me, "I'm going to bring in some fresh stuff from home."

He was a man of his word. Sure enough, he showed up the very next day with an armload of magazines and began arranging them neatly around the waiting area. Again, I made an attempt at light conversation only to be ignored. I figured that he was a dyed-in-the-wool loner but you would think he would at least have the courtesy to acknowledge my inquiries, however briefly.

"It's a good thing I have Rad for company," I commented to Karen. "Robert isn't very much fun."

Karen and I thought perhaps Robert was married since we occasionally saw him walking toward the clinic with a well-dressed, auburn-haired woman. She never came in but waited patiently either outside the front door of the clinic or in the car. I knew by his past responses not to ask him if he was married, so I told him about my wife, Karen. It was like speaking to a brick wall. I thought, "I'm going to see this man every day for at least another month, providing one of us doesn't die during this process." On a gut level I felt that Robert was too shocked and scared to deal with someone else's problems, let alone his own. So another day and treatment passed and he remained silent.

After another week, I could see the treatments were taking their toll on Robert, just as they were doing to me. Robert was the kind of person who would show up an hour early rather than be a minute late, so we had a lot of inequality time together. That is to say, the staff would stop in to visit with Rad and myself, primarily to check out Rad's outfits that Karen was now changing on a regular basis. Unfortunately, Robert's sour personality and grumpy countenance caused most people to steer clear of him. While lying on the metal table that was still warm from Robert's body, I tried to think of some way to comfort him as they strapped me to the table and placed that confining mask to my upper body. "I really wish Robert would open up and come out of his shell," I mused. "Rad has always been a great icebreaker. Maybe my goofy green frog can get through to him."

The next day I took up my usual post with Rad in the chair next to me. Inspiration struck and I moved Rad to my knee facing Robert. I nudged Rad a bit, just short of bouncing him up and down like I did with my grandchildren. Finally, Robert looked at me and then at Rad and back at me again and said, "OK…

What's up with the frog?" There must have been a smile on my face a mile wide as I heard Bogart's final line from <u>Casablanca</u> in the back of my mind, "…[T]his could be the beginning of a beautiful friendship."

And it was.

GETTING THE FEEDING TUBE

Soon I found myself in the middle of cancer treatment. Five days a week I was pinned to the table by that confining mask over my face and upper body. Fighting back claustrophobic panic and struggling to breathe through my teeth, I tried to pray: "Please, Father, help me be still. Let it be over. Make it stop hurting." A huge machine that reminded me of the metal monsters from <u>War of the Worlds</u> whirled around my head, emitting a constant hum like an X-ray machine. It stared down at me through finger-shaped lashes that revealed, then concealed, its insect-like compound eye for up to two minutes before moving to search for the next place to fry.

The treatment caused the worst case of "dry mouth" you can imagine. My tongue cracked and my gums and cheeks were as dry and blistered as if I had been licking the felt on a pool table. My voice became very scratchy and froggy. I carried a water bottle everywhere to provide the moisture in my mouth because my body could no longer do it. But swallow? Forget it.

Each successive treatment burned more and more throat tissue. Once when I was caught without my water bottle companion, I began gagging from dry throat convulsions. We were driving down the interstate searching for an exit. Karen watched my struggles with increasing concern. "Do you want me to spit in your mouth?" she asked. I know it sounds weird – and a little gross – but it really was a very kind offer. And, no she didn't have to, we found an exit. But we never got into a car again without several bottles of water on hand.

Early in the game the doctor had warned me that I would probably need a feeding tube. "Not me!" I thought. "I know a guy who went through this without the tube. If he could do it, so can I." Brave words until you've gone five days without food and are pushing three without water. I don't know what I was thinking, but once you can't swallow any more, it's time for the old feeding tube trick. At that point, I was delirious from dehydration anyway, so they didn't get much of an argument from me. Karen drove me to the doctor's office on a Thursday. We made the arrangements in a hurry for Friday morning surgery. The upcoming weekend was the three-day Memorial Day weekend. The doctor didn't think I could wait four more days to have the tube inserted.

I woke up in the hospital room with a new hole in my stomach. Karen was in the room with me when Dr. Bell came in to check on me. I was groggy but feeling better since they had pumped a couple banana bags of fluids through my IV. I must have looked less shriveled, too. The doctor looked me in the eye and smiled. "It's amazing how fast the body bounces back when you get fluids and electrolytes back up," he said, obviously pleased with my improvement.

I looked across the room at him and said a bit peevishly, "I have a son about your age."

After silently checking the placement of the feeding tube and the circulation in my feet, Dr. Bell tweaked my big toe and responded, "I have a father about your age."

Rad just smirked at me from his perch across the room.

Rest, fluids and the feeding tube were working wonders – wonders being relative when you're being treated for cancer. But I was getting impatient. I was lucky that Dr. Bell was able to do the surgery before the holiday weekend, but now I was getting anxious to get out of the hospital. I was scheduled to go on a church retreat – the Walk to Emmaus – the following weekend. I discovered that getting out of a hospital on a three-day weekend was harder than getting in. When Dr. Bell finally agreed to sign me out, it was late Sunday afternoon.

I don't know about other people but I rest better in my own bed. I had wanted as much rest as possible at home before the retreat began on Thursday evening, just four days after I was released from the hospital.

WALK TO EMMAUS

"Then the two from Emmaus told their story of how Jesus had appeared to them as they were walking along the road, and how they had recognized him as he was breaking the bread." Luke 24:35 (New Living Translation).

The trip from Jerusalem to Emmaus was seven miles. After the crucifixion, two of Jesus' followers were joined by Jesus on their walk to Emmaus. They walked those seven miles with him but they didn't recognize him at first. Do angels walk among us, protect us and guide us on our journey? Do you feel the presence of the Holy Spirit in prayer or see the hand of God in your child's eyes? I didn't recognize who was walking with me at first either.

ERIC'S WALK

The Walk to Emmaus – what is that? Now I know it as a deeply spiritual experience, an experience my church family was anxious for me to have. But back then I only knew it was a retreat of some sort that a lot of my church friends had gone on. You know, another one of those "church things" like Christmas and Easter but not as well known. At that time it wasn't a church function I wanted to attend. It was something I needed to get out of the way. My friends kept telling me how great it was and how I should go. So I said okay. The one good thing about the three-day "walk" is you're only allowed to do it once. So I thought once I get this out of the way, it's done. Then I can go back to church once a week and read the Bible as needed and life goes on – or does it?

So I had signed up for this Emmaus thing in January 2004, knowing I didn't have to go on the walk until June. I also signed up my son, Eric. I mean, he could use some religion. Who knows, maybe something will come up and I won't have to go. Now that's something to pray about. As luck would have it, I was out of town working and couldn't be released to attend the walk. Later I discovered luck had nothing to do with it, it was a God thing. A number of people called me to see if they could talk me into coming home, but I was adamant. This place would fall apart if I left. I would postpone and go next year.

My only concern was that Eric might not go if I didn't, and I just knew that he really needed this more than I did. So I talked to my son, Eric. He assured me he would go anyway. With a smile on my face, I felt as if I killed two birds with one stone. I got out of the Walk and pointed my son in the right spiritual direction. But little did I know that was God's plan, not mine. Eric had to go on the Walk first so he could lead me through mine.

Yes, I had signed up to attend the Walk the following summer, the summer of my cancer nightmare. I was in the middle of treatments when the time came for my Walk to Emmaus. I had an even better excuse to get out of it that time, but by then I very much wanted to go.

MY WALK

I felt I had something going for me – the power of prayer. With the number of cards, e-mails, letters, friends and church family members, there must have been hundreds...no, with the other churches around the country...thousands of prayers. "With that kind of support," I thought, " I will F.R.O.G."

With cancer, you have a good day or a bad day; there were no mediocre days for me. On a good day I made it out of bed, as opposed to a bad day when I vomited blood and writhed in pain. Even with the encouragement of prayers, there was no way I would have three good days in a row to make the Walk to Emmaus. The pain was out of control even with hydrocodone, oxycodone, oxycontin, fentanyl, morphine and ibuprofen by the handful. I began to have doubts about my ability to attend the Emmaus Walk. Karen wouldn't be there to grind up the pills to place in the feeding tube and I didn't have the strength to do it. Who would be there to rip off my shoes to massage my big toes and/or massage my cheek bones in an attempt to control the violent vomiting brought on by radiation poisoning and drugs? I couldn't imagine how I was going to get through this. But by then I had learned that the answer was to leave it up to God.

God had already prepared the answer to my concerns. I was going on this retreat as a pilgrim. But there would be others in attendance to guide and serve the pilgrims. There would be speakers and leaders and a group called "the cooks." Yes, they would be cooking for the pilgrims but they also took care of all of the pilgrims' other needs. Only previous pilgrims can be cooks and they must attend preparatory training sessions. My son Eric had signed up to be a cook for my pilgrim group and had completed all of the training. Because of my special circumstances, Eric was assigned to be my cook. And although the cooks usually sleep in separate quarters, he was allowed to stay with me to be my caregiver and drive me to the clinic for treatment. God had a purpose in sending Eric to the Emmaus Walk that I couldn't make. Those who had previously bemoaned the fact that I was unable to make the original Walk now saw that God's timing is perfect. So I let go and let God and began my walk in Faith.

I was no longer just reading the Bible, I was studying it. For the first time, I was praying directly to the Holy Spirit who was always with me. I had never felt His presence until now. I was no longer praying outwardly to our Lord with hands clasped and mind focused on the sky. Once I accepted Christ, He took up residence in my heart and soul. I now turn my prayers inward towards the Prince of my being who dwells within me.

"… it is no longer I who live, but Christ lives in me; and the life which I now live in the flesh I live by faith in the Son of God, who loved me and gave Himself up for me." Galatians 2:20

A very good friend gave me a card that said, "Courage is fear that has said its prayers." Well, I was saying my prayers fervently. Now that I know life in Christ, my fear of life without God is neither life nor death but hell. I said that cancer may be a cure for sin. It can also be what sentences us to everlasting life rather than certain death. DO NOT look to miracles to prove your faith in God, look within at your soul.

"God's light is truly brighter than cancer's shadow." Lynn Eib, <u>When God and Cancer Meet</u>.

During my Walk, the group had provided a cot for me to lie on for those "sit down, fall down, and now lay down" moments that had plagued me throughout this trial. I still managed to sit at the tables for six of the fourteen hours of prayer, worship and testimonials. At night I slept on a sofa with my son, Eric, on a cot next to me. We were away from the group in a small room that provided privacy for the tube feeding, tube medicating and inevitable vomiting. Although I carried an empty two-gallon ice cream bucket and a wet wash cloth everywhere, surprisingly I only needed it in the privacy of that room.

During one of the evening services the Emmaus group asked if they could pray over me. Knowing the power of prayer, I consented readily. I was very humbled by their request. What a gracious gift…to be prayed over by my brothers and offered to our Father in Heaven as a blessing in faith. When we gathered in the sanctuary, they placed me in a chair at the foot of the altar. The closest began to place their hands on me while the remainder of those gathering placed their hands on one another creating a continual chain of touch. As the group began to pray, I wanted to tell them, "DO NOT pray over me for healing, but rather, pray with me for God's salvation. DO NOT be disappointed if God does not heal me."

When praying for the sick and dying, we should first ask the Lord to cleanse sins from the soul. Unwittingly, out of selfishness we often ask Jesus to restore our friend or family member's health and neglect their soul. We are the last line of defense and I will tackle Satan before I allow him to steal your soul. Please do the same for me. *"..and the prayer offered in faith will restore the one who is sick, and the Lord will raise him up, and if he has committed sins, they will be forgiven him." James 5:15*

That group prayer was very uplifting, deeply moving, yet utterly humbling, all at the same time.

Meanwhile, unbeknownst to me, my son, Eric, was standing on a chair in the back of the sanctuary observing the prayer gathering.

Now this may seem rather odd so I should explain. Eric runs the sound system at our church, the same church that hosted this particular Walk to Emmaus. In the course of his duties, he occasionally needs to stand on his chair behind the soundboard in the back of the celebration hall to be able to evaluate the needs of the worship team on the dais in front of the altar. During his first Christmas Eve Candlelight Service in this capacity, he began what became a yearly tradition for him. He would stand on his chair during the candle lighting ceremony and singing of "Silent Night." I had no idea what he got out of this practice until he invited me to join him last Christmas Eve. Like an eager child, I stood on a chair next to my son sharing that marvelous experience, not as father and son but as one in the Lord.

So during this particular gathering of the Emmaus fellowship, Eric had retreated to his familiar perch. Later that evening, Eric told me what he had observed during this united act of prayer. As the Emmaus group prayed over me, the group had assembled themselves into the shape of a cross.

COMMUNION BY PROXY

On June 4, 2005 the Walk to Emmaus #155 was gathered in the sanctuary for prayer and Holy Sacraments. When the group was invited to partake of the Holy Communion, I remained seated with my head bowed in prayer. My irradiated throat was so ravaged I knew that I couldn't swallow water let alone the Holy Sacraments of Christ Jesus. Then I felt a strong but steady hand on my shoulder. As I slowly raised my head, my eyes saw an aura around the hand upon my shoulder. I felt a gentle tug and my friend, Ron Pitt, said, "Come with me, Michael."

He was encouraging me to come with him to the altar and receive the Holy Sacraments. I closed my eyes and slowly moved my head back and forth gesturing no. But Ron remained resolute. As he lifted me to my feet, I pleaded in a croaking whisper, "I can't! I can't even swallow water!" But we walked together down the aisle, Ron steadying me with one arm.

Meanwhile, my mind was frantic; I had no idea what was going to happen at the Lord's Table. When the Body of Christ was offered to me for the forgiveness of my sins, I reached out and took a very small piece. "Maybe I can just keep it in my mouth until after communion," was my thought. "Just try not to choke!"

As I dipped the bread into the grape juice it became the Blood and Body of Christ. Then, in a gesture of pure compassion, Ron reached for my hand holding the Host and moved it toward his lips. With his other hand, he took the Holy Sacrament from me and placed it in his mouth. My eyes filled with tears as Ron and I were united in oneness with God. Communion by proxy! On the following Sundays my son Eric would do the same in turn.

"I relieved his shoulder of the burden, His hands were freed from the basket." Psalm 81:6

After three days, my Emmaus Walk was coming to an end… or should I say the beginning of the never ending "4th day" of my Walk with Christ. I stood before the congregation and proclaimed that I was now going to go about Mary's work. I had done my share of Martha's work as president of the Board of Trustees, finance committee member, administrative council member, usher, plumber, electrician and janitor at Trinity Heights Church. Now I was going to learn how to pray and preach the gospel. And, as Saint Francis of Assisi urged, I would "use words if necessary."

"...I get tongue-tied, and my words get tangled." Exodus 4:10 (New Living Translation)

KAREN'S WALK TO EMMAUS

The Emmaus pilgrimages are usually scheduled with a women's Walk immediately following the men's. So one week after I began my Walk to Emmaus, it was my wife's turn to begin her Walk. My sister, Pam, agreed to stay in our home to care for me in Karen's absence because I could no longer care for myself. Even with a feeding tube, the weight was falling off of me. Anticipating this downside of the radiation treatment, Karen had fattened me up to 213 pounds before my treatment began. By this time I was down to 165 pounds. Dr. Bowens admonished me, "Sometimes old people quit eating and die." I recognized that as his well-intentioned but undiplomatic method of trying to encourage me to eat. But just about everything that went into the feeding tube came back out with a vengeance.

At this point, I felt that I was in a death spiral that I couldn't pull out of. I had also reached the point where I wasn't able to sleep. Karen was worried as she prepared to leave for her Walk to Emmaus retreat. However, I assured her I would be fine under my sister's care. So Karen went to join her Emmaus group on a Thursday afternoon.

I had been to see the doctor about my insomnia and he had prescribed Ambien. "Finally!" I thought. "Blessed sleep at last!" After throwing up the first round of meds, I crushed a second sleeping pill and poured it in the feeding tube. That time it stayed down. Sleep finally came to me. Sleep so deep that I awoke to the horrible reality that I had lost control of my bodily functions. I was covered from head to toe with feces. The sheets were a mess and I was a mess. My entire body, the feeding tube… even my face…was covered. I was too sick and embarrassed to burden my sister with my shame. But I was far too weak to help myself. I remember trembling with tearless weeping as I stood in front of the mirror reaching with both hands towards Heaven. I closed my eyes and cried out to the Holy Spirit, "MY LORD, MY FATHER, MY GOD, HELP ME!!" *"In my distress I called upon the LORD, And cried to my God for help; He heard my voice out of His temple, And my cry for help before Him came into His ears." Psalm 18:6*

After that, I don't remember a thing until the next morning when I woke up to clean sheets and a clean body. I thought for an instant that it all had been a horrible, cruel dream. However, when I went into the bathroom, I spotted the soiled sheets and clothing in a neat pile on the bathroom floor. I knew I didn't have enough strength to clean myself up, much less change the sheets.

My sister slept in the downstairs bedroom during her stay. After I had staggered downstairs to put the sheets in the washer, I found her sitting in the living room sipping her coffee. I asked her, "Did I keep you up last night?"

She peered over the rim of her cup and replied, "Nope, didn't hear a thing after you went to bed."

I know I experienced a miracle that night. There's no other way to explain it. This was no dream or hallucination; I put the physical evidence in the washer with my own hands. My sister was oblivious. I was physically incapable of helping myself. Perhaps those seven angels that I recognized during my hypnosis lifted me up and washed me clean. All I know, with the utmost certainty, is that I cried out to my Father and He answered me in my hour of abject need.

TIME CAPSULE

The doctor had been honest when he warned me, "You're going to start feeling better when we start the radiation. That's because the treatment will start killing the cancer which has been making you feel so bad. About a week to ten days into it, the radiation itself will start making you feel worse. Unfortunately, that doesn't stop until well after the treatment is over." He was right on the money. The radiation treatments were dragging me farther and farther down. But thanks to the feeding tube, I soon had enough strength to lie in bed and feel sorry for myself.

On one particular day I was thinking about our cat, Axel, a big, puffy seal point Himalayan with dreamy, sky-blue eyes. His brother, Raistlin, died the day before we arrived home from Pensacola. The two had been with us together for sixteen years and, once we were home, Axel began walking around the house crying. He mourned his brother for three days before settling down.

Like so many pets with an almost psychic connection to their owners, Axel knew something was wrong with me. He was always the more demonstrative of the two cats, often curling up on our laps in the evening. He was an equal opportunity cat, sharing his affection with both Karen and me, but after we returned, he became inordinately attached to me. He followed me around the house and lay on my lap for hours, just being near me. I couldn't complain; he was very comforting. But when I was no longer able to eat, Axel stopped eating too. I told him

I had a feeding tube – as if reasoning with a cat ever did any good…but he still refused to eat. Karen tempted him with bacon and chicken and other favorites, all in vain. He eventually became too weak to walk and we agreed that we should help him cross the "Rainbow Bridge." Our son, Eric, drove Karen and Axel to the vet's office and then buried him with his favorite toy next to his brother. Karen cried inconsolably during the entire trip. I stayed at home, too weak to go with them and too sick to cry for my beloved companion. His loss couldn't have come at a worse time. I was so sick that I thought I was going to die but afraid I wouldn't.

So there I was, lying in my bed wallowing in self-pity, when I heard a Voice in my room. It was loud and clear, speaking to me, directing me. "Go to your underwear drawer. Retrieve something for Me."

I didn't recognize the Voice at that time. But this was the same Voice I would hear later when the Holy Spirit plucked me from near death and said, "I have work for you to do." It didn't occur to me that this might be the Voice of God. I was under the impression that if the Lord God ever talked to me through the Holy Spirit, my head would explode or I would be paralyzed with fright. But it didn't, and I wasn't.

I didn't know what was happening but I couldn't refuse the command. So I rummaged through the drawer where I keep my underwear and socks at the urging of the Voice. I came across a bottle bag from Bangkok, Thailand, a rosary from my Catholic youth, a photo of Karen in her late teens. Then, under my Vietnam service medals, I found a little book with a dark blue leatherette cover – a pocket devotional titled <u>My Imitation of</u>

Christ by Thomas à Kempis. The moment I touched it, I felt a jolt go through me as if an arrow had hit its mark. I knew that this was what I was meant to find. I had forgotten it was even there, but when I saw it, the memory flooded back. I remembered my mother giving it to me over twenty years ago. At that time I hadn't even opened it. I just thanked her for it, kissed her, brought it home and tossed it in the drawer with my other special treasures.

I opened the book to the first page. It had my mother's name, E. Ruth Bradford, with a handwritten inscription: "To – My dearest son Michael Gary, love, Mother." She had also written a message to me: "I pray that this book will give you as much consolation as it has always given me." Beneath that message she added, "Page 259 sure does help." The Voice had sent me to receive a message from my mother written some twenty-plus years earlier and brought to me long after her death. It was a message to me written by my mother, but inspired by the mind of God to be stored away for today's need.

As I was thumbing through the book to page 259, I wondered what message the Lord had sent to me. The left page, number 258, had an illustration depicting a man with head bowed and hands folded in prayer.

Page 259 began Chapter 29, titled *"How God Is to Be Invoked and Blessed In the Time of Tribulation."* Several passages had been underlined by my mother:

> Blessed, O Lord, be Thy name forever.
> Who hast been pleased that this trial and
> tribulation should come upon me." – DAN.III.26.
> I cannot fly from it, but must of necessity fly to
> Thee that Thou mayest help me, and turn it to my
> good.

Lord, I am now in tribulation, and my heart is not
at ease; but I am much afflicted with my present
suffering.
And now, dear Father, what can I say? I am
caught, O Lord, in straitened circumstances: O
save me from this hour. – JOHN XII.27.
But for this reason I came unto this hour,
that Thou mightst be glorified when I shall be
exceedingly humbled and delivered by Thee.
May it please Thee, O Lord, to deliver me; for,
poor wretch that I am, what can I do and whither
shall I go without Thee? – PS. CVIII.21[1].
<u>Give me patience, O Lord, at this time also.</u>
<u>Help me, O my God, and I will not fear how
much soever I may be oppressed.</u>
...And now, in the midst of these things, what
shall I say? Lord, Thy will be done – MATT.VI.10.

I closed the book and held it to my heart praying that I would
be able to hold fast on the course that lay before me. *"Blessed is
a man who perseveres under trial; for once he has been approved, he
will receive the crown of life which the Lord has promised to those
who love Him." James 1:12*

This encounter with the Holy Spirit was a turning point in my
faith. Now I could trust that God was with me and I began to
cling to Him as my source of strength.

***

During this time of trial, I received other messages from loved
ones who had passed beyond, one of whom was my grandmother.

---

1   à Kempis, Thomas, *My Imitation of Christ/*revised translation, Confraternity
     of the Precious Blood, Brooklyn, NY, 1954. (Please note that the reference
     to Psalm 108:21 is part of the original text although there is no 21st verse to
     Psalm 108.)

My grandmother, Irene Jeffries, died of throat cancer when I was less than two years old. My mother told me how she held me up outside the window of my grandmother's room. It was the only way she could see me since small children weren't allowed in the wards with terminally ill patients.

Fifty-five years ago, cancer treatment was mostly experimental. Doctors were using surgery to remove cancerous tissue and were experimenting with radiation on inoperable cancers. My grandmother, Irene, was approached with the idea of experimenting with mustard gas on throat cancer. During WWI mustard gas caused extreme burning and destruction of throat and lung tissue, in most cases resulting in death. Doctors thought, if they could use small amounts of this gas on Irene's throat, they might be able to burn and destroy just the cancer cells. My grandmother agreed to the procedure, stating her hope that this may be able to help others. I cannot fathom the incredible amount of pain this woman must have endured before succumbing to death.

Fifty-five years later, I found myself in incredible pain from throat cancer and burning radiation treatments. My sister, Pam, was looking through Grandma's Bible and found a prayer and message Grandma had written during her cancer treatment. Knowing the pain and suffering I was going through, Pam reasoned that if I had this prayer from my grandmother during her suffering, it would help me in mine. No one in the family was aware of the existence of this prayer until Pam stumbled across it in Grandma's Bible. Pam doesn't recall why she was looking through the old Bible, but I suspect that she was being directed by the Holy Spirit.

> I do not ask a truce,
> With life's Incessant pain;
> But school my lips, O Lord,
> Not to complain.

I do not ask for peace,
From life's eternal sorrow;
But give me courage, Lord
To fight tomorrow.

"Suffering is not something to merely endure.
Out of it we are to build a Cathedral of heavenly
beauty; and in that Cathedral we bring to God,
our deepest devotion. The pain which endures,
the frustration which we never escape, the meager
and tepid life which is to be ours always; these are
the bricks from which we are to build with never
ending diligence and faithfulness, the loveliest
worship, devotion and faith, which is permitted
men to have."

Irene H. Jeffries

Irredeemable Abyss

Around the middle of May, I realized I couldn't drive anymore due to drug-induced dementia. There were times I didn't know who, where, or even what I was. I was horrified when I returned to reality with the full knowledge of what had just taken place. I could remember the terror of not knowing that I was a human being on the planet Earth.

As my condition continued to deteriorate, I also began to experience what I called "sit down or fall down moments." When this happened, I had no choice. I had to sit down immediately or I was going to fall down. It didn't matter where I was...in a grocery store, the doctor's office, or the mall – I would suddenly just sit on whatever object was closest. One minute Karen would be walking with me then she would turn around to find me sitting on a furniture display, a palette of dog food, a planter, or even the floor.

Even with my immune system shot, I still managed to make it to church and maintain my duties as an usher. That small act of service to the Lord meant so much to me. I must have thought that while ushering I would be exempt from the "sit down or fall down" phenomenon, but there were no exemptions. One Sunday after passing the offering plates, I fell in the back of the church. As the brass plates hit the floor, it sounded to me as if the bell choir's table had just fallen over. In reality it wasn't that loud, but several people turned around to see what had happened. As I was attempting to get back on my feet and gather the scattered plates, I noticed my good friend, Cathy Johnston, turned in her seat and looking back at me. She began to cry. I wanted to cry too because I knew I couldn't usher any more, but I was too sick to cry. That's right. I could no longer do Martha's work and I hadn't even begun Mary's yet. As my uncle used to say, "Cheer up things could be worse." So I cheered up and, sure enough, things got worse.

As another side effect of the treatments, my mind would race from topic to topic like a bipolar sufferer in their manic phase. Kind of like what you've been putting up with while reading this. I asked a brother in faith to pray with me and for me. He assured me that he prays for me every day. In desperation, I said, "No! You don't understand. My mind is racing so fast that I can't concentrate on prayer." At this point he clutched my hands and assured me that the Holy Spirit prays for me when I'm unable to.

"In the same way the Spirit also helps our weakness; for we do not know how to pray as we should, but the Spirit Himself intercedes for us with groanings too deep for words; and He who searches the hearts

knows what the mind of the Spirit is, because He intercedes for the saints according to the will of God." Romans 8:26-27

This newfound knowledge was an enormous comfort to me during these dark times. And it was something I needed to learn in order to help others who faced similar trials.

***

The downward spiral now continued at an accelerated pace as my condition deteriorated further. I had gone into this battle against cancer with both guns blazing. Now, with no fight left, I just wanted to die in my own bed at home. Karen continued to encourage me, to read to me and she prayed and prayed. When the cancer was first diagnosed, it was in the late-first/early-second stage. Doctors don't like to give numbers or percentages but they gave me an eight in ten chance of beating this thing. But I had reached the point where I began to suspect I might be one of the two in ten that would lose this battle.

I was ready to give up. Like Elijah, I had come to a juniper tree, sat down under it and prayed that I would die. *"...It is enough; now, O LORD, take my life, for I am not better than my fathers." 1 Kings 19:4*

Again, Karen gave me some of her strength and courage. She must have ground thousands of pills, measured doses of meds, washed me, rubbed my toes and cheeks to control the vomiting, rubbed my back to induce relaxation, and applied lotions to cracked skin. Then she read to me and prayed over me. It's hell being the patient but I can't imagine the stress, anxiety, and helplessness of the caregiver. I was a tremendous drain on her mentally and physically, not to mention the terrible drain of her energy, for I had very little of my own left. As I grew weaker, I had to spend more time in bed. The "sit down or fall down" continued with increasing frequency. Like a runaway locomotive, my mind found an even higher gear and was covering eight to ten subjects a minute. Poor Karen, she couldn't keep up and I had a hard time slowing down. I would leap from one thing to another even when I tried to stay focused.

Finally, I hit the wall in my woeful, wretched struggle against this bitter foe known as cancer. The proverbial saying that the cure can be worse than the disease is an understatement. In the beginning, I vanquished all my fears through prayer, but now with no fight left in me, I succumbed. I was imprisoned in my body with the disease and tortured by the medical warfare that attempted to drive out the demon. Thirty-two cancer treatments had annihilated my body and vanquished my will to live.

FATHER, SON & HOLY SPIRIT

Whenever I was in route to the cancer center for an appointment and treatment, my mind wandered and rambled to any place but there. I thought I'd rather be headed to the dentist…even the proctologist for a hemorrhoidectomy… No wait, I closed my eyes and I'd gone fishing. No matter how you look at it, the cancer center is an endless drag for both the sick and healthy. After my brother, Greg, was treated for prostate cancer, he told me that he will drive miles out of his way to avoid being anywhere near the incredible pain, suffering and general uncertainty that exist behind those walls.

The burn-out rate must be extremely high for the technicians and staff at the Center. While I was a patient, I found some of the staff to be cold and mechanical. Perhaps they were shielding themselves from emotional involvement with us to avoid the pain of losing a person who had become more than a name with a face. The ones who dared to reach out and touch the individual living soul within us are true disciples of their trade.

The power of one's faith is an everlasting factor in the way you live and die. Despite the glorious news that the doctor was reducing the number of treatments I would take by three, I still had five to go. I informed my wife Karen that I refused to take the last five radiation treatments because I would no longer subject myself to false hope and unrelenting pain. Karen cajoled, "Please, Michael. One on Thursday and one more on Friday. Then you'll have the weekend. You usually gain some strength back over the weekend." After repeated pleas from my wife and children, I agreed to two more treatments.

But when Monday arrived, I once again vehemently refused the last three treatments. Karen reminded me, "This is the only chance you have to kill this thing. The doctor says they can never use radiation on you again." Even Karen's supplications wouldn't change my mind. Even sick unto death I could be pretty stubborn.

Shakily holding three fingers up towards my face she implored quietly but firmly, "You have three treatments left. You won't do it for me; you won't do it for your children; you won't do it for yourself. Okay," she said counting off the three fingers she held in front of me. "Then do one for The Father, one for The Son, and one for The Holy Spirit!"

How could I refuse?

"so that the proof of your faith, being more precious than gold which is perishable, even though tested by fire, may be found to result

in praise and glory and honor at the revelation of Jesus Christ."
1 Peter 1:7

Several months later I asked Karen, "How did you know to say the only words that would convince me to complete the treatments?"

"I didn't come up with the Trinity as an argument. He did!" she responded pointing skyward.

IRREDEEMABLE ABYSS 2

When the treatments were over, the pain wasn't. It was as if the workers had burned out the interior of the structure then departed, leaving a huge heat lamp burning in the empty shell. Nothing seemed to ease the pain. Fentanyl did, but it suppressed my breathing to the point that I had to gasp for breath. The last thing they used was liquid morphine. Karen had to keep a chart and make notes indicating times and dosages to prevent an overdose.

It would be very easy to overdose with liquid morphine. I understand how patients undergoing lengthy and painful courses of treatment must question the desirability of living. I know my brother, Greg, did.

Sometime during my own cancer treatments I learned that Greg had undergone radiation treatments for prostate cancer. When he was diagnosed, Greg instructed his wife, Cathy, to tell no one: not his four children, not his sister, not his church family, and not me, his only living brother. He tried to continue his life as if nothing had changed. But a really big change was about to happen. The disease and its treatment fraught with pain finally took their toll on him, draining the very essence of life from mind and limb. He discontinued the cancer treatments. Shortly thereafter he drove out into the woods and took an overdose of painkillers. Then the Lord spoke to him and said, "You will not take your life." With the Holy Spirit at his side and the voice of God in his ears, he immediately drove himself home and purged the drugs from his stomach.

The Lord saved Greg's soul from eternal damnation just as He had mine. Had it not been for the hope engendered by the rekindling of my faith when the Holy Spirit sent me to look for my mother's prayer book, I might have been tempted to embrace an "accidental" overdose myself.

However, while I would not take my own life, I had lost the will to live. Sure I had made it through the treatments, but even with medication the pain was still present under the muffling haze of the drugs themselves. I had blood blisters in my mouth; my throat burned incessantly; every breath, cough or sneeze was excruciating. All this time I had been going through the motions of reading the Bible and prayer, but still the difference was between knowing and believing. Knowing is in the head while believing is in the heart and soul. I believed with all my remaining strength, mind, heart and soul that I was a child of God but I prayed to be released from the relentless suffering.

After three days of not knowing what was going on, certain bodily functions were shutting down. I had lapsed into the depths of a semiconscious state. I'm not sure whether it was all the drugs or the horrendous toll exacted by the unrelenting pain. I had now sunk as low as I had ever been, emptied of the essence of life. I was in limbo, neither alive nor dead. I folded in my struggle and embraced, even welcomed, death. As a child of God, I prayed to my Father, "I can't endure this relentless suffering. You have forsaken me. Just let me go. Let the pain end."

Before cancer, I was so full of my work, family, friends, and myself that there was very little room for God. I figured I would make room for Him in my life later when I had more time. There will always be more time, won't there? But since I wasn't making room for Him, He created the void so there would be room for me to grow in spirit. I believe the Lord heard all of the prayers that were being raised on my behalf. He let me get as empty as I could possibly be and then said, "OK, let's take another look at my child."

I was lying in bed beside Karen expecting the angel of death when I felt strong arms grasp me around my chest. I was lifted out of my bed and set upright on my feet. In front of me, where the bedroom wall and fireplace should have been, I saw bright clouds moving and swirling in space. Then, I heard a loud voice say, "I have work for you to do." I recognized that Voice. I had heard it once before. Then the supporting arms were gone. Somewhat befuddled I looked at the bedside clock: it was 2:15 a.m. Then I quickly turned to look at Karen. The Voice was so loud; surely she should have been awakened. I had just been physically lifted out of bed; surely she should have been disturbed. But she was still lying there sound asleep. As I stood there on wobbly legs, I heard a soft whispering, quite different in tone and volume than the loud voice that had awakened me. I was instructed, "Put food in your feeding tube. You will not throw it up." Suddenly the resplendent, tumbling clouds faded and became the mundane bedroom wall and cold fireplace.

Despite limbs trembling from weakness I slowly made my way downstairs to the kitchen. I retrieved a can of liquid nutrients and returned to our bedroom, plopped myself down beside the bed and, as instructed, poured the contents into my feeding tube.

That was the turning point in my recovery. I began to regain strength. The pain subsided ever so slowly. But I now believed that God wanted me to live and I wanted to live. I've been working for the Holy Spirit ever since.

MIRACLES

Throughout my struggles there were instances when prayer was answered so immediately that there could be no other explanation for what had happened. I knew that my prayers were being answered, as well as those of the many friends, relatives, and even faith-filled strangers.

At the beginning of the radiation treatment the oncologist, instructed me to make an appointment with my dentist. While the oncologist oversaw the actual radiation treatments, I would need a dentist to monitor the effects of the radiation on my teeth and jaw.

The news was far from encouraging. My dentist, Dr. Wilder, confirmed the oncologist's prediction that I would probably lose my salivary glands. This meant I would have to wet my mouth with a bottle of water every twenty minutes for the rest of my life, day and night. He also said it was highly probable I would lose my teeth and possibly my lower jaw.

Dr. Wilder loaded me up with a variety of gels, rinses, and brushes and very specific instructions about caring for my teeth during the treatment. He also explained that once tooth loss began I would need to go to Phoenix where I would be placed in a hyperbaric chamber to prevent infection. He said I could be in the chamber for several days possibly up to a month.

During the six weeks of radiation my salivary glands stopped functioning. I experimented with various oral moisture gels and artificial saliva, but in the end I just carried a water bottle with me everywhere. I kept a glass of water on my night stand for the many times I awakened at night. I asked the oncologist and my dentist and the ENT if there was any chance I might regain salivary function. They were all hopelessly pessimistic. "After this long it's highly unlikely."

Despite three doctors advising me that my salivary glands were history, I wouldn't give up on prayer. So I prayed, "My Lord, my Father, my God," as I took a sip of water. "I will only pray this prayer for twenty-four hours. Every time I take a sip of water, I will pray for You to return the function of my salivary glands."

After four months, the big mucus glands kicked in. I thought I was going to choke on their sudden bounty. A few days later the little glands around my front teeth began to resume their duties. I could whistle if I wanted too. Within a few more days the BIG, honking, hamburger-eating, lemon-squirting ones kicked in... HALLELUJAH!!

Every three months for the next two years Dr. Wilder would say, "You shouldn't have a tooth in your head – your mandible is dead." Sure, my teeth got real loose and wiggled all over the place for a while. But I still have teeth because the Lord wants me to tell everyone that I have them through the power of prayer.

It was over two years later and Dr. Wilder had retired. My new dentist, Dr. Benton, shook his head in amazement and said, "Salivary glands don't come back."

I told him, "You can see that they do. Through the power of prayer I have my teeth."

Then Dr. Benton confided, "My brother is undergoing cancer treatment right now. He's lost his salivary glands."

I gave Dr. Benton a little stuffed frog to give to his brother. About eight inches high, it sported a fishing hat and vest, and carried a fishing pole. Around its neck was a nametag that said, "F.R.O.G. – Fully Rely On God" on the front. On the back of the tag was this quote from Mark 1:17: *"Follow Me, and I will make you become fishers of men."*

Whenever I give anyone a frog, I always tell them that my frog reminds me to pray. I have frogs all over my house. Most of them are gifts from friends who know how prayer has changed my life.

***

Toward the end of the treatments my doctors were trying various drugs to relieve the pain. I had a severe reaction to one of these medications which resulted in a violent seizure. During the worst of it, Karen had to lay her body across mine in an attempt to prevent injury from the spasmodic thrashing of my arms and legs. During a lull in my thrashing Karen called the doctor's office. Of course it was after hours, so the answering service paged the on-call physician. Unfortunately, it was not my doctor so he was unfamiliar with my history. "Okay, if it doesn't stop in another hour or two, call me back."

Well, it stopped at about the two hour mark. I was exhausted and just went to sleep for the night. But the next morning I woke up with blurred vision in my left eye. I was able to get in to see my ophthalmologist, Dr. Rivers, that same morning. He examined me and explained, "During your seizure a small blood vessel burst in your left eye. The seeping blood blurred your vision. I'll have to send you to a retina specialist, but his nearest office is in Prescott."

I was told Dr. Strauss is renowned in his field. After only one encounter, I began to affectionately refer to him as Dr. House in deference to his outstanding bedside manner. Karen and I had driven many miles to his office in Prescott, Arizona. We waited for what seemed an inordinately long time before I was taken in for a variety of tests. Then back to waiting…this time in the hall between the lobby and the testing area. Finally Dr. Strauss appeared, sailing swiftly down the hall towards us. He paused abruptly where we were sitting and bluntly informed me, "Your retina is so severely damaged that you'll probably be permanently blind in your left eye. There's nothing I can do for you." Then he continued to sail on down the hall, leaving Karen and me to stare at each other dumbfounded before we gathered ourselves and began the long drive home.

That night during prayer I thanked my Father for the vision in my right eye and for fifty-six years of vision with my left. And believe me, I was sincerely grateful. However, I continued my prayer, "Father, if You can see fit, would You please return the sight to my left eye." And in the morning, I could see with both eyes. I went to Dr. Rivers' office to inform him my sight was restored. After calling Dr. Strauss's office and running several quick tests, Dr. Rivers summoned another doctor and several nurses into his office and proclaimed, "Look at these results. The only explanation for the return of this man's sight is a miracle brought about through the power of prayer."

I heartily concurred. This is NOT ABOUT ME. It's about our Lord and Savior and the power of prayer through the Holy Spirit.

WEIRD OF HEARING

Throughout this cancerous storm, our lifeboat had been held up by the hands of prayer and guided by faith. Karen and I had not been prepared for the tsunami that was destined to cause my little boat to turn turtle. With the first set of waves, I had been told to prepare for the loss of my saliva glands along with all of my teeth. Then I had been unexpectedly broad sided by the rogue wave of the seizure that caused the loss of sight in my left eye.

Still the power of prayer proved mightier than the turmoil found in the sea of life. The mounting waves cleansed the sins from my soul and lifted my spirit heavenward. Praise God! The waves started to subside as the tide stopped coming in, and I believed I could stand firm.

The relentless pain in my throat began to ease a bit, although I still had the residual cancer headache in the center of my forehead. Then amid the apparent cessation of the waves, I began to hear a faint ringing sensation in both ears. Within days the ringing became a low roar, followed by dizziness, vertigo and nausea.

The tsunami wasn't over, so I climbed back into life's boat and made an appointment with Dr. Bowens. The ringing soon turned to a swishing sensation. With each and every heartbeat, I could hear the rhythmic and synchronous pulsing of my blood swooshing through the jugular and carotid arteries in my head.

"How annoying," I thought, "but at least I know my heart is beating because I can hear it and that means I'm alive."

I don't remember much about the ensuing office visits to determine if the swooshing sound I was hearing could be caused by micro-vascular compression syndrome, pulsatile or vascular tinnitus. All I know is that zero hour was rapidly approaching; this cruel, unrelenting swooshing sound with ever increasing volume was on the verge of becoming intolerable.

Dr. Bowens discussed several theories, the details of which I don't remember. He talked about swelling and blockage causing arterial turbulence as a result of radiation therapy. I have since read that a high-riding jugular bleb causes blood vessels and arteries to become positioned closer to the hearing portion of the ear than usual. After two weeks I figured I was on the verge of my own "China syndrome," which would be a meltdown where my brain poured out onto the ground.

Dr. Bowens scheduled me for surgery. He would check for tumors or other anomalies and either implant an endolymphatic shunt or perform some kind of decompression procedure.

The waves continued to grow in size and began breaking over the bow of my boat, but again the stretched-out hands of prayer steadied her and placed me in calmer waters of faith. The day prior to surgery, the angry sea was like a mad dog frothing at the mouth as the tsunami mounted a second wave, gobbling the remains of the first. The ceaseless tumult from listening to my heart beat for two weeks was vexing…even maddening. I began to despair of ever finding safe harbor.

That night when I went to bed, my mind was roiling with the possible outcomes from tomorrow's surgery. I could scarcely pray while waiting for the sleeping pills to kick in. I don't know what I prayed for that night but I do know what I will pray tonight.

"He makes me to lie down in green pastures: he leads me beside the still waters." Psalm 23:2 (English Standard Version)

I awoke to a calm sea of blessed quietness; the only sound I heard was my sigh of relief as I took a deep breath and gave thanks to the Lord for lifting this impetuous doom from me.

"…you have been distressed by various trials, so that the proof of your faith, being more precious than gold which is perishable, even though tested by fire, may be found to result in praise and glory and honor at the revelation of Jesus Christ." 1 Peter 1:6–7

I called Dr. Bowens' office to let them know I would not be in need of his services that day. I hung up the phone and knew I would be in His service as I began to pray in peaceful calm and quiet.

***

My vision has been returned to my left eye, all my teeth remain, along with a wet tongue and a smile for my saliva glands, and my taste buds are back. Until now, no one knew what took place in our lifeboat except for those who lifted it in prayer and the Lord, for He calmed the sea. When the next storm comes, go to your lifeboat (friends), and ask them to lift you up in prayer while our Father calms the sea. You don't have to wait for a storm to pray for your friends and loved ones. On calm seas even a faint whisper can be heard.

Does prayer work? Perhaps you will say, "yes" if your prayers are answered the way *you* want them to be answered. Perhaps you will say, "no" if God's answer was not what you prayed for or expected. We don't know the final plan. What we pray for today, we may not necessarily want tomorrow.

God has a plan so let go and let God.

"For I know the plans I have for you," declares the LORD, "plans to prosper you and not to harm you, plans to give you hope and a future." Jeremiah 29:11 (New International Version)

The secret to talking with God is to remember, it's not a one-way conversation. You must listen. More than once I was told, "I gave you two ears and one mouth." I have learned that our time and our Lord's time are not equal. When our prayers are not answered according to our request, is God listening? OF COURSE!

Are you praying? Do you believe in Satan? *You'd better.* He believes in you.

Climbing Higher

Every August in Flagstaff the American Cancer Society holds its annual fundraiser, Climb the Mountain to Conquer Cancer. Although I had read about it in the local newspaper, I had never participated in the event. A few months prior to my diagnosis, a friend had invited me to join a climb team called Covenant which is made up of several local churches. I had signed up, but I didn't know if I would be able to make the 2005 climb, coming as it did so soon after my treatment.

After the climb, I wrote about the experience. That story follows.

CLIMBING THE MOUNTAIN ... 2005

How do you climb a mountain? ONE STEP AT A TIME. With faith and hope one can pursue and overcome most of what life throws at us. While undergoing cancer treatments, I dreamed of climbing the San Francisco Peaks with thousands of others in Flagstaff, Arizona's annual "Climb the Mountain to Conquer Cancer." Sponsored by the American Cancer Society, the walk begins in a parking area on the lower end of the road to Snow Bowl Ski area. The seven-mile walk begins at an altitude of about seven thousand feet and ends at the ski lodge some two thousand feet higher. Buses are provided for the participants who crater when their bodies hit the wall of physical endurance.

Karen and I had signed up to participate in the climb before I engaged in mortal combat with cancer, a crusade I would have lost if not for the power of the Holy Spirit. Five weeks after my brush with death, I prepared to ascend the arduous path carrying my stuffed F.R.O.G. – Fully Rely On God, named Rad in a small backpack. That morning he was all decked out in his little shirt and pants and sporting a breast cancer survival hat, nametag and purple HOPE ribbon. This stuffed F.R.O.G., about eighteen inches high with large eyes and grin to match, had been a constant reminder to me that the Holy Spirit is with me always and to pray without ceasing. Rad had accompanied me to thirty-seven cancer treatments, over a hundred doctors' appointments, two surgeries, and battles against two types of cancer. That's why this F.R.O.G. got a free ride to a critical destination – my salvation – and I pray that many others will learn to F.R.O.G. I can still see the smile on my friend's face as he says, "That's a mighty fine-looking F.R.O.G. you have there, mister."

It was a late August Saturday morning when our good friend, Martha Green, arrived at our home at 6:00 a.m. to drive us to the starting line for the Cancer Society's walk. Martha had double knee replacement several months earlier and she still had considerable swelling. We were all excited at the prospect of encouraging others to fight this disease that destroys the very host that sustains it… YOU. It was just after 7:00 a.m. when I strapped on the backpack that held Rad. I grabbed a bottle of water, said a prayer and started up the mountain with Martha on my right and Karen my left. It was a beautiful, clear, crisp morning but we knew it was going to warm up fast as we made our way up the winding road through Ponderosa pines, aspens and gambel oaks.

We proceeded at a gradual, determined lumbering pace. Rad doesn't talk, but that morning – forgive the hyperbole – he was knockin' 'em dead. Facing backwards with his arms open wide and that frogfish smile of his, Rad had a chance to greet most of the climbers since we were passed by just about everyone, each smiling in turn and waving after seeing my goofy F.R.O.G..

We made it past the first mile marker and then the second, each with tables offering water, juice, brownies, and fruit pieces to sustain the walkers and runners. The thought crossed my mind that I could crush up the brownie with fruit pieces and poke the entire concoction down my feeding tube.

We made the halfway point! Hey, what happened to mile marker three? The buses coming up the mountain made an occasional stop for a hero that had to abandon their quest to conquer the mountain. With the gust of a second wind, we realized there was a good chance we would make it.

It was mile five and about four hours when I heard "CLICK-CLICK" behind me. Oh NO! It was the F.R.O.G. paparazzi wanting to know why Rad was making the trip up the mountain in my backpack. His story hit the papers the next day, "EXTRA! EXTRA! Michael makes a slow but steady pace up the mountain in the walk to conquer cancer with his stuffed frog Rad in a backpack." The newspaper even printed the real story that F.R.O.G. stands for "Fully Rely On God."

Next came a mile of encouragement as we approached a large curve at the beginning of a huge aspen grove. There along the side of the road were placards bearing the names and photos of those who waged war against cancer. I had lived to fight another day. But others were still engaged in mortal combat. Some had lost that fight but had won the love of Christ Jesus.

Our mutual friend Judy, who had passed us earlier, doubled back and joined us during that last mile with support and encouragement. Each step had become painstaking and the air was a bit thin as we approached nine thousand feet in altitude. Martha and I would stop to occasionally embrace, grab each other's hand, and then take one more determined step. We were all encouraging others on the road with increased enthusiasm as we neared the end of our trek.

We finally approached the top. Suddenly just around the corner and out of sight came loud cheers. It turned out to be the Northern Arizona University Cheerleading Squad. The climbers were greeted as heroes, and I suppose we are.

The Outback restaurant provided a barbeque lunch at the Lodge, and there was a tent for cancer survivors and their families. Karen and Martha got their barbeque plates as I found a quiet corner of the tent where I removed a can of formula from Rad's backpack and poured it into my feeding tube.

The following year we all made the trip again, this time in a little over four hours rather than six. Oh, and thanks, Outback, for my barbeque. I didn't write about that climb. But this event was becoming a tradition for Karen and me.

By August 2007 I was planning to make the climb for the third time. Karen had signed up. too. but she would be riding one of the buses to the top to meet me, having broken her ankle during one of our training hikes. I teased her, "If you didn't want to make the climb, all you had to do was say so."

I told Karen that during these climbs I pray for the growing number of friends and family who have been touched by the demon cancer. I felt as if I were carrying each one of them up the mountain with me in spirit. Then Karen found a way for me to physically demonstrate that sentiment; she made iron-on patches with the names of those I was honoring with my climb and attached them to my official climb T-shirt.

After the 2007 climb, I wrote the following addendum to my 2005 commentary on the climb:

Continuation ... 2007

Along with three thousand nine hundred and ninety-nine others, Rad makes his third trip up the mountain in my backpack. Karen was unable to accompany me, having broken a bone in her ankle when she fell while training for the climb. As I climbed the mountain, I offered a prayer with every step, lifting up prayers for those suffering, those departed and the elusory cure. Challenging the mountain can be exhausting, as is the struggle with cancer itself. Sick and weary, you long to utter a cry of submission and give yourself over to tears and abandon hope. I will not let you yield; for I will carry your name in my heart and your spirit with my soul up the mountain in prayer. I am not immune to your fears, pain and suffering. Through a covenant with you, I will share your burdens and lift them up to the Lord.

Continuing up the mountain with dogged determination, the pack stretched out with the youth moving ahead of the aged and the well encouraging the sick. Struggling for air and looking for that elusive second wind, I was passed by a smiling woman in her mid to late sixties who informed me she lost half of one lung to cancer.

The second wind just kicked in as a little of my own self-pity flew up the mountain. I presented F.R.O.G.s of encouragement to several of God's children, young and old. I told them to Fully Rely On God and when they look upon their goofy smiling frog, let that be a reminder to pray to the Holy Spirit who is always with them. I made it to the top that day with help from your spirit and the wings of angels.

After the climb, Karen created greeting cards with a photo of me carrying Rad in his backpack for a cover. She cut the patches out of my shirt and glued them inside the card with a Bible verse and an explanation of what the patch symbolized. We mailed the cards to the cancer survivors or the families of those who had succumbed. I included a printed copy of "Climbing the Mountain – 2005" with the "Continuation – 2007" in the hope that it would give encouragement and bring peace to these precious people.

The patches on the shirt and the cards after the climb have become a part of the climb tradition. This is the 2008 letter that went out with our cards.

AMERICAN CANCER SOCIETY 40TH YEAR

CLIMB THE MOUNTAIN TO CONQUER CANCER 2008

I was looking forward to celebrating two anniversaries. This year, Karen and I celebrated our 40th wedding anniversary in July, and the American Cancer Society celebrated 40 years of fund raising through their Climb the Mountain to Conquer Cancer event in August. This would be our fourth trip up the Mountain in three years and a reminder that I still have two more years until I am officially in remission. Just like climbing the Mountain, it's not easy battling cancer. There's always that shadow hovering over you. I am still fighting and I won't let cancer win.

The month prior to the climb, I hadn't been feeling well. I'd had fevers, drenching night sweats, swollen lymph nodes in my neck and groin along with a sore throat and headaches. That's the way it is with cancer. Every ache, every pain, every swelling – is it the cancer coming back? I'm not a hypochondriac but you must remain vigilant against this thief that's always lurking in the shadows. And it's not just me. My fellow survivors have assured me they keep a watchful eye and wonder with every new ache or symptom. It is not just the fear of death. It's mostly the fear of the pain of cancer and the even worse pain inflicted by the treatments.

My doctor tried several rounds of antibiotics to rule out bacterial infection or other more common afflictions. Then my neck swelled up so that it looked like one of those cartoon ostriches that had swallowed a golf ball. By the time I got in to see the doctor, the swelling had gone down. He scoped my throat one more time but saw nothing to indicate a return of the tumor in my throat. He told me ominously, "Well you definitely don't have squamous cell. The symptoms you're describing are non-Hodgkin's lymphoma. I'll order a PET scan." My heart sank.

In route to radiology, we stopped first at our church for prayer. Pastor Karol, Julie Vlieg and Karen prayed with me and over me. They anointed my head with oil and cloaked me in prayer. Then we went on to the hospital – Rad in the back seat and Karen in the front. When we arrived, a dear friend and brother in Christ, who serves as a chaplain at the hospital, met us in the waiting room. When I approached the receptionist, she beamed up at me, "I remember you and your frog!" I smiled back and asked, "Do you remember what FROG stands for?" "Don't tell me!" she cautioned. With a gasp and a thoughtful look at the ceiling, "Fully Rely On God!" she exclaimed triumphantly. Our friend just looked at me, smiled and nodded affirmatively.

The waiting room was just about full; however, there were three seats in the corner. After Karen and I took our seats, the chaplain approached us, squatted down, grasped our hands to form a circle and began to pray in a soothing voice, loud enough to be heard by all in the waiting room. As his confident voice pronounced the promises God has made to us and asked for his mercy on me, I began to feel a sense of hope and relief as the frightening symptoms melted away. I know this prayer was offered up to our Father for all of His children in the waiting room.

After the prayer, I began chatting with a young woman sitting next to me. Karen was conversing with the chaplain, but my attention was focused on my sister in Christ. She was also there for cancer screening. While holding Rad on my lap, I began to tell her about my frog, how he got his name and what he means to me. At the same time, I couldn't help but notice a white-haired woman with twinkling eyes looking intensely at Rad from across the room. Holding Rad up, I looked directly at her and asked, "Do you want to see my frog?" She stood up and walked across the room smiling mischievously. I thought she wanted to see Rad but she leaned past me and addressed my wife. "You know, through the years, I've had men ask me if I'd like to see a variety of things. But none has ever asked me if I'd like to see his frog." About that time, her husband was called by the nurse and she turned to escort him. But not before she and my wife shared a conspiratorial chuckle. I just sat there abashed, with my ears turning red.

The PET scan went smoothly and within a few days I received the good news that there was no sign of cancer. What a glorious and triumphant banner to take with me on the climb! After receiving our T-shirts from The American Cancer Society, Karen began to make a list of names for all those we would pray for while climbing the Mountain. She then transferred the names to white iron-on patches on both of our shirts. For the families, we also carry the names of those who lost their battle against cancer. I lost my older brother eight years ago Christmas morning and his widow had recently succumbed to cancer herself. Karen placed their names on each of my shoulders. My prayers are empathetic and pure for those struggling with cancer, their families, and the families who've lost loved ones.

Early on the morning of the climb we caught the first shuttle at the high school that would take us to the starting point for the walk. Rad was already in his backpack, dressed for the trip. After getting off the bus, Karen and I headed over to the sign-in desk and asked the woman staffing the position to snap our picture. Later on, back home, when we downloaded the photo, Karen noticed a man in the background. Ironically, I would have a lengthy conversation with that man, Andy, during the hike up the mountain.

We were grateful that it was cool and there was a light cloud cover on the mountain that morning. An occasional dark cloud would spit a few droplets of tears on us as a reminder why we were there. The sun can be very intense at high altitudes and Flagstaff was in full summer mode right then, with temperatures breaking eighty almost every day. Later on towards the top of the mountain, the sun finally broke through the clouds and the sky turned to a deep cobalt blue as it does at that altitude.

You meet a lot of people on the hike. Some walk very slowly, while others jog past at an athletic pace. Children glide by in strollers while others ride in backpacks (like Rad), or perched on shoulders. You pass some and some pass you. We would chat with the volunteers at the water and snack stations and commiserate with those in the long lines while waiting to share the port-a-johns spaced somewhat sparsely along the route.

Every person on the walk carried their own personal burdens and –yes, joys. Some had just begun their battle without wavering or halting, despite difficulties or setbacks; others had overcome the enemy. Some carried the memories of loved ones departed; others held onto and prayed for their loved ones currently tangled in cancer's web. Cancer is totally dispassionate about who it will strike. It can come to anyone: the very young, the very old, and anyone in between.

Climbing with me I saw faces black, white, yellow, red and brown – the whole beautiful rainbow of colors God has chosen for his children – proof that no race or nation is safe. A grey-haired Navajo woman walked proudly with her staff to steady her. She was wearing her climb T-shirt over her traditional tiered skirt; her two grandchildren scurried ahead then returned to her. She told of a brother taken by the disease. Two women of far-eastern descent walked together, the older one wearing a sari, her younger companion in a T-shirt and black denim capris. A slim black man in a dashiki shirt walked alone.

I stopped to chat with Pastor Karol, who was handing out snacks at the water stop staffed by the Covenant Churches. A lively young woman detoured toward me as she was jogging by. "What does FROG stand for again?" she asked. "Fully Rely On God." "Thanks!" she hollers as she jogs off up the mountain. Pastor Karol looked at me and smiled.

Remember the mystery man from our photo at the beginning of the walk? I met him again in the picnic area at the top. His name is Andy. He told me that he has fought cancer three times. Then he assured me, "And I know what F.R.O.G. stands for." One of the volunteers overheard our conversation. He told me his 14-year-old daughter is a survivor, having had leukemia when she was four. I told him my F.R.O.G. story and gave him a stuffed frog to give to his brave daughter. He became very emotional, and while he fought back his tears, I heard the indistinct utterance of the word "God."

This event is the major fundraising event of the year for the American Cancer Society. But that's only one reason I do it. It's also a way for me to honor the dear ones who have been touched by this terrifying disease. But most of all, I love telling the story of hope and how F.R.O.G. sustained me through the valley of the shadow of cancer. If my story helps just one person, it's worth every step I take on that mountain. And I am deeply heartened when someone remembers…Fully Rely On God.

Part 2

Divine Appointments

DIVINE APPOINTMENTS

HURRICANE 1...KATRINA

On August 28, 2005 Hurricane Katrina, a powerful category four storm, was crouched in the Gulf of Mexico, threatening the coast from Louisiana to the Florida panhandle. Karen and I had been home since March when we left Pensacola, Florida and the work on Hurricane Ivan. A week after we arrived home, I was diagnosed with cancer. Karen had used her allotted "down time," emergency family sick leave, and a large chunk of vacation time to care for me during the five months of cancer treatment and recovery.

With Katrina bearing down on the Big Easy and the "Redneck Riviera," Karen's company needed all of their specialized catastrophe workers on call. Karen's remaining vacation was cancelled and her manager placed her on standby. There would be no more time off for her to care for me. It was time to go back to work so we both began packing for the long haul.

Katrina slammed ashore in the vicinity of Slidell, Louisiana with a catastrophic storm surge, affecting everything from Bay St. Louis and Gulfport to Biloxi. Everything was either destroyed or uninhabitable up to a quarter mile inland from the beach.

Although I still had a feeding tube in place, my doctor gave me the okay to return to work on a limited basis if I promised to have my scheduled follow-up in mid-September. He told me he would find a doctor for me in the work locale if I didn't come back to see him. I promised compliance and set out.

Car packed to the brim and a case of liquid food for my feeding tube on the back seat, I drove to Phoenix with Karen. From there she flew to Birmingham, Alabama where she would rendezvous with her fellow managers to receive her deployment instructions. After I dropped Karen off at the Phoenix airport, I pointed the car east on I-10 toward Mississippi with divine guidance as my map.

The next day Karen called to give me an update. "My team is being dispatched to Biloxi, but I'm not going with them." The adjusters she supervised were like family to her, so I knew it would be hard for her to send them off without her.

"Why would they do that?" I asked.

"Well, Steve (her boss) really wanted me to go to Biloxi with the team. But I told him that you were driving out to meet me," she explained. "Don't take this wrong. He's glad you're coming out and understands how important this is to both of us. But he's concerned because it's so soon after your treatment. He knows your immune system's been compromised. The Gulf Coast is a mess." I could just imagine! We had lived in Biloxi during two Air Force assignments and I remembered what Hurricanes Camille and Frederick had done to the area. Karen continued, "Steve's concerned about the sanitary conditions in the area, the lack of housing and potable water. It'll be a challenge for healthy folks, so he's worried that it might adversely affect your health."

She paused, "He's right, you know. They need a team manager in Jackson so he's sending me there. Call and let me know when you get closer. I should have an office location or hotel room by then." I adjusted my route to take me into Jackson.

***

Still several hours out of Jackson, I stopped for gas then enjoyed a beautiful sunset while I poured a can of "go-juice" in the feeding tube. I continued to follow the beam from the Spiritual Lighthouse on toward Jackson, pondering a probable shortage of hotel rooms due to the million evacuees that had fled New Orleans and the coastal areas in Katrina's wake. As I looked down at Rad sitting in the front passenger seat next to my Bible, I knew that I could F.R.O.G. to get me safely into Jackson.

Jackson, Mississippi, City of Grace and Benevolence, at last! But when I stopped for directions, it became apparent I was in grave danger. Jackson's population of one hundred and eighty thousand had doubled in the last three days. The police department and the infrastructure were stretched to the max. Gasoline and housing were next to nonexistent as residents and refugees competed for scarce resources.

I found myself lost in the worst part of town. I had stopped for directions at a convenience store where long lines of folks were attempting to get gas and other dire necessities. I got out of my car and approached a middle-aged black man for directions to the nearest lodging. He took my elbow, spun me around and began walking me back to my car. He whispered to me urgently, "You're not safe here! I'll walk you to your car…get in, lock the door, turn right out of the store parking lot and left at the light, go five miles and don't stop for anything." As he closed my car door behind me, my guardian angel turned to face a small group of dour-visaged adolescent black men who were headed towards my vehicle. He detained them long enough for me to make my escape. I suppose at this point, if I had four flat tires I would have driven on the rims for that five-mile stretch.

The electricity was still out in some parts of town and the roadsides were strewn with vehicles that had simply run out of gas, abandoned where they stopped, their windows now shattered. My mind turned to thoughts and prayers for the folks in New Orleans and along the Mississippi Gulf Coast. What violent pain and suffering had taken place and was still going on in the areas that had been annihilated by the powerful storm? I looked up the street and saw the lights from a familiar sign, "Wendy's Old Fashioned Hamburgers."

I wasn't able to eat food by mouth, but I felt safe enough to stop for directions to a hotel. "Besides," I thought, "my guardian angel might be having a burger." I approached a young lady in line and inquired about accommodations. She said that she and her mother had just checked in to a large hotel which was partially hidden around the block behind Wendy's. Out of the hundreds of motels and hotels in Jackson, this turned out to be the very hotel at which Karen's company had made reservations for us the following night.

Tired and with some difficulty, I managed to locate the hotel. They were booked, but the front desk was able to find me a room for the night just a few miles down the road. Then I contacted Karen who would be driving a rental car from Birmingham to Jackson in the morning. I told her to make sure she gassed up well before Jackson. Gasoline was so scarce tanker trucks received a police escort on the road and while they were unloading at the stations.

In the morning I located the facility that would be used as the catastrophe office. I introduced myself to the folks in the vanguard who were expecting me and began setting up telecommunication and office equipment needed by the teams and their management. While moving the heavy equipment and boxes of printer paper, I began bleeding around the feeding tube entrance to my stomach. John, who was the Computer Automation Procedure Specialist (CAPS), noticed the blood on my shirt and asked me, "They told us you would be doing light work for us. What part of 'light work' don't you understand?"

I thought to myself, "I have to get rid of this tube ASAP." But thanks to swelling, blisters and burning, I was still not able to eat most solid foods. I made a prayerful vow with God and myself that I would consume all foods by mouth starting now no matter what the pain, which turned out to be considerable.

I remembered two weeks earlier when I tried solid food for the first time. Karen fixed me a cup of chicken noodle soup and I chewed it slowly because my jaw hurt from lack of use. The first spoonful went down hard and tasted awful because my taste buds had been damaged by radiation. Karen went upstairs to work on medical bills as I forced down another painful spoonful. All of a sudden, my stomach realized it had bits of something solid in it for the first time in three months. A distress signal went out from my stomach to my brain, "MAY DAY!" as acid poured into my stomach. I called out in a panic to Karen, "HELP ME – HELP ME!" as I grabbed my stomach. Karen attempted to get Maalox and Pepto-Bismol down me but it was too late. The reverse gear was in motion. Karen reached for a wet washcloth and massaged my cheeks. But I did better with each successive attempt at solid food.

Conditions were not ideal in Jackson. The refugee population crowded the hotels and motels. There were long lines in restaurants at all hours of the day, and vendors frequently ran out of gasoline and food. All of us were working long hours and living in hotel rooms. But the strength of faith in that office lightened our tasks and our moods.

We settled into the standard routine of working seven to seven, six days a week. I got to know my co-workers in the small area where we provided clerical and IT support for the operation. They were all people of deep faith so I shared my story of cancer, salvation, and F.R.O.G. with them. My story was met with tears of joy or a quietly whispered, "Amen."

It turned out that John had a story too. He had volunteered for this assignment temporarily. Normally he worked regular hours out of an office in California; and on his weekends, he served as an itinerant pastor for several small rural towns near his home. He brought several of his sermons to work for me, and then Karen and I read them at night in our room.

Battle Dress!

It wasn't always easy to keep my mind focused on God and the good he had done in me throughout my struggles with cancer. On many occasions I found myself beset by Satan.

Every member of the clergy, everyone who preaches the gospel of Christ Jesus, and His followers are subject to repeated attacks from Satan. These attacks are cleverly disguised and are atrociously wicked. This fallen angel has the power to torture our bodies with diseases and incite spiritual corruption. Acknowledging his power to do harm is not meant to give the supreme evil spirit any accreditation, but rather to admonish believers of his enmity against God. As Christians, we are in the middle of this struggle with the Antichrist but there are ways to fend off his unrelenting attacks.

Jesus was of the flesh and was constantly tempted by Satan. *"And He was in the wilderness forty days being tempted by Satan; and He was with the wild beasts, and the angels were ministering to Him." Mark 1:13* Jesus was able to remain without sin with the full knowledge of His Father; he knew the future and "angels were ministering to Him." How can we, with our mortal limits of understanding, fight Satan's malevolent designs to destroy our relationship with God?

Satan doesn't waste his time with the souls that he knows are 'in the bag.' With vigilance, the bête noire seeks those closest to his most feared enemy, our Lord and Savior. So how do we defend ourselves against a malevolent foe as conniving and powerful as Satan?

While I was still under treatment, a close friend sent me to Ephesians 6:13-17 which teaches us how to defend ourselves against Satan's flaming arrows:

"Therefore put on the full armor of God, so that when the day of evil comes, you may be able to stand your ground, and after you have done everything, to stand. Stand firm then, with the belt of truth buckled around your waist, with the breastplate of righteousness in place, and with your feet fitted with the readiness that comes from the gospel of peace. In addition to all this, take up the shield of faith, with which you can extinguish all the flaming arrows of the evil one. Take the helmet of salvation and the sword of the Spirit, which is the word of God." Ephesians 6:13-17 (New International Version)

The struggle between good and evil is unrelenting and we are often caught with our shield down. Words like "Christ Jesus," "come Holy Spirit," "Lord God Almighty," "Lord of Lords," "King of Kings," "the blood of Christ," "my Father in heaven" along with the power of prayer can thwart Satan's attack. Satan does not need any enticement to come to you but he can be repelled with the words "go from me." The strength of your faith will summon more frequent and violent attacks.

Temptation

I had made a promise to my ENT in Flagstaff; it had been three months since my last checkup and it was time to see if cancer – like a thief in the night – had crept back and was lurking in the shadows. Karen made an appointment with an ENT doctor in Jackson and, as always, accompanied me to my appointment. Karen was with me for all doctors, therapy, PET and bone scans, blood tests and general checkups since that day I came home and informed her I had cancer. I know that my best friend and wife will be with me to combat any affliction or additional attacks of cancer or Satan himself.

I can't begin to tell you what a comfort it is to have someone walk with you every step of the way through this period of trials and tribulations. I can't imagine how anyone does it alone. And of course, The Holy Spirit is there to guide and protect me when all the emotions of anger and self-pity and, with willpower weakened, Satan's attempts step in.

When he taught me about the full armor of God, I told my friend that the light from Satan's flaming arrows will light my way down the footpath toward Heaven.

To someone battling cancer, there is no such thing as a routine test. I remember Karen asking a radiation tech if she could sit and read the Bible with me after I was injected with a large dose of radioactive glucose for a PET scan. The tech replied, "Ma'am, you don't want to be anywhere near this man right now," as he slowly closed the door to the lead shielded room.

So there we were in the car headed for an appointment with some ENT doctor in a strange town and I was full of anger... even rage...and self-pity. I was waging a war against Satan and he was winning. All the things I had been taught about how to protect myself flew right out the window with an ever-increasing speed, exceeding that of the vehicle's, as we drew closer to the doctor's office. With profanity in my mouth and hands pounding on the steering wheel, I protested that I did not want to go before some judge and jury, that is, some doctor who would pass sentence over me by telling me whether I would live or die, or get a temporary stay of execution.

Karen just sat very quietly as I continued to act out as a child throwing a tantrum because I had to go to the doctor's office. After a couple of wrong turns, we finally located the hospital with the doctor's office next door. I remember turning the car engine off and staring at Karen in defiance. I put on a pretty good pouting performance, silently daring her to say something. Why was I not able to name the names of the Lord to drive off this wicked stench of vileness? Satan doesn't waste time on the souls that belong to him but he adamantly pursues the ones that turn to the Lord. Why was I not able to take up the full armor of God and vehemently resist this foray by Satan? Was I also being led by the Spirit to be tempted by the Devil? (See Matthew 4:1)

Upon entering the doctor's office, the receptionist presented me with a fistful of medical history and insurance forms attached to a clipboard and, with a smile, asked me to complete and sign all forms. I promptly passed this mess to Karen and began digging in my jeans hip pocket for my wallet and insurance card. Karen began filling out all the forms as I sat there with my fingers clasped together over my mouth, legs spread with elbows planted defiantly on my knees. I was throwing a real doozy of a pity party. But soon I started to get bored with it because nobody was buying into it and I was growing weary.

I glanced around at the people in the waiting room so I could ascertain the approximate waiting time, and I became curious about a rather nice-looking woman who was holding a laced handkerchief with both hands, creating a covering over the lower half of her face. I tried not to gawk. I assumed that maybe she was covering her face to avoid germs, because nothing else about her attire suggested she was Muslim. She was engaged in an unintelligible conversation with a young man in his mid to late twenties whom I assumed was her son. Absorbed in my daydream, I barely noticed as one corner of her shroud slipped from her fingers. She quickly retrieved her veil of dignity, but not before revealing a horrific sight. The now unveiled angel was attempting to conceal the fact that part of her lower jaw was gone, leaving a gaping hole in her face down to her neck. I gasped inside, ashamed beyond words for previously acting like a petulant child.

As this divine messenger restored her veil, I closed my eyes in prayer to ask comfort for her and forgiveness for me. I asked the Holy Spirit to teach me how to pray for this suffering soul. A calming peace came over me as the Holy Spirit spoke. "Look upon my innocent daughter as a child running with the sun on her curly hair, playing, laughing and smiling JUST AS I SEE HER."

I prayed fervently, "I believe that prayers offered to the Lord are his and can never be revoked. If in prayer I could offer up to You, Lord, all those that had been said on my behalf, I would give them to you for this your innocent daughter, my sister. Amen."

Several months later, in the waiting area of another hospital in another city, I assisted a woman with chestnut hair who was suffering from degenerative rheumatoid arthritis. She had the classic "Z-Thumb" symptom and swans-neck deformities of both hands. There were painful looking knots protruding from her knees and ankles and she was unable to walk without assistance. I later told Karen, "I now have two little girls on my prayer list."

The ENT examined me, had tests run and passed judgment: no change. I inquired about the possibility of having the feeding tube removed. I had been eating all meals by mouth now. The ENT gave us the name of a gastroenterologist and we scheduled an appointment two weeks down the road to make sure I no longer relied on the tube. I figured they could go in, deflate the bulb in my stomach and remove the tube. It turned out not to be that easy.

During my lunch hour I was admitted as an outpatient to the hospital in Jackson to have the feeding tube removed. When the doctor came in, she started explaining the removal procedure. Basically she said, "I'll wrap the tube around one hand, press down on your stomach with the other, and pull the tube retainer through stomach wall and abdominal muscles. It's going to hurt real bad for about ten seconds." I looked closely at the doctor's face. She wasn't smiling and she didn't appear to be some kind of sick-o that derived some morbid pleasure from this, so I thanked her for being honest and above board with me. Okay, she painted this somewhat gruesome picture and, yes, I did believe this was going to really, really hurt. However, I hadn't realized until then that the tube retainer was a piece of rigid plastic as big around as a quarter and just under an inch long.

After confirming that my wife wasn't squeamish about blood, the doctor instructed Karen to stand behind me and hold one arm over my head while the nurse held the other. Oh Boy! She continued with, "Take a deep breath and start letting it out slowly. I'll count to three and you try to relax." By now I was about as relaxed as an iron man with two six packs of steel for abs. ONE, TWO, THREE…YOWL!!! It felt like I had been shot from the inside out with a 9mm Glock as the full-metal jacketed bulb the size of my thumb flew out of me like an extraterrestrial. As I counted the ten seconds of extreme pain in my head, I looked down at the hole in my stomach that slowly began to close as the doctor began applying pressure to the wound. The pain gradually subsided to a bad burning sensation as she dressed my boo-boo. She told me not to eat anything for two hours since I might leak and suggested I consider taking the rest of the day off. No way was I going to sit around the hotel feeling sorry for myself. I was going back to work where others could join in feeling sorry for me.

I returned to work after a lighter than usual lunch, which had resulted in only minor leakage. My coworkers expressed surprise and then dismay that I hadn't taken the rest of the day off. The dismay was followed with secretive scurrying and an apparent follow-up call to the florist so the delivery could be moved up to that afternoon. Then my coworkers presented me with a floral arrangement in a smiley faced coffee mug. I spent the rest of the day surrounded by the warm emotions and silent prayers of genuinely kind people.

Before I shut down my computer for the day, I checked on the newcomer to the Gulf of Mexico…a monster named Rita. Packing winds 175 MPH, this strong category five was the third most intense ever to hit the Gulf of Mexico. With resources already stretched for Katrina, we knew that someone would be leaving Jackson after Rita made landfall.

HURRICANE 2 – RITA

On September 24, 2005, Hurricane Rita made landfall near Sabine Pass, Texas. Now a strong category three, she pushed a twenty-foot storm surge into the southwestern Louisiana coast. Rita would turn out to be the meanest storm in years. In Louisiana the community of Holly Beach was totally destroyed, and other small towns in Cameron Parish virtually disappeared, while the city of Lake Charles literally became a lake. The initial death toll was over one hundred, and two million residents lost electricity. Beaumont, the largest city in southeast Texas at 118,000 plus, was extremely hard hit. It was spared the storm surge, but Rita indiscriminately twisted anything she didn't blow away.

The call came for us to leave Jackson. We were headed for Houston to prepare for work in Beaumont. We were on the road by noon, headed south. We carefully mapped our way to slip north of ruined New Orleans and catch I-10 just east of Baton Rouge. As we traveled, we passed convoy after convoy of power company trucks going our way at their lumbering pace. In Beaumont alone, it would take power company crews from all over the United States more than three months to restore power, with the help of twenty thousand electricians and five thousand trucks.

We stopped just after dark in Lafayette where Karen's brother Keith lived. By staying with him, we didn't have to worry about a hotel and we could check on conditions further west. Along the road gas stations had been crowded, closed or out of gas. But well before dawn, Keith led me to a sure source of gasoline on a back road so I could fill up before we headed towards Lake Charles.

It was still an hour before sunrise when we headed west again on I-10. The rural landscape was pitch-black except for an occasional light at a home that had a generator. In the early twilight, we approached Lake Charles. We could barely see hints of watery destruction on either side of the highway. We had to travel through the city on the business loop because the big bridge on I-10 was closed. All exits from the highway were blocked by National Guard troops.

In another hour we were in Beaumont. Other than the first rays of dawn, the only light was from the generator-operated flood lights that the National Guard had set up at the exits on I-10 and occasional passing car headlights. It was eerie and unsettling to see ghost images of large trees and power poles downed across homes and businesses in the dim purple light of predawn. As we proceeded towards Houston, I wondered what the Lord had in mind for us.

We checked in at the main office in north Houston. Although we would be working in Beaumont, we were told to check into a nearby hotel. Then we drove a hundred miles back to Beaumont with papers that would allow us past the checkpoints set up by the Guard.

A vacant grocery store had been rented in Beaumont for a temporary office, so we could be close to the area we were serving and the people we were there to help. Power was provided by a huge generator the size of a semi-trailer. Three satellite dishes provided communication lines for telephones and computers. Folding tables equipped with telephones and Ethernet lines became work stations for the two hundred plus adjusters who would work the claims and the managers who would direct the work. File cabinets, fax machines, desktop computers and printers filled the area occupied by the support personnel. A large open work space and smaller areas for reception, storage, meetings and dining had been created by hanging huge sheets of black plastic from the ceiling. Dismal décor, but functional.

Our makeshift office was across the street from a Mexican restaurant which, like most businesses in the area, was closed due to the widespread power outage. Like sensible people, the owners had cleaned out their refrigerated units as soon as they were allowed back into the area. Spoiling food can permanently ruin the unit in which it is stored. Having done what they could to prevent any further damage to their business, the owners waited for power to be restored and for some sense of normalcy to be established before beginning the task of reopening the business. Unfortunately for those of us working across the street from the restaurant, the work crew had dumped the spoiled food in the dumpsters next to the restaurant – and there were no garbage pickups being provided by the city. The stench became over-whelming after a few weeks of warm autumn weather. When we were downwind, we would run for the door to the office with cloths over our noses. Eventually the city managed to conduct garbage pickups at restaurants and grocery stores, but it took quite a while for the air to lose the smell of rotting organic mat-ter and stagnant water. After the restaurant reopened, Karen and I couldn't bring ourselves to eat there despite reports that the food was quite good.

Since no restaurants were open, the company initially provided MRE's (military grade "meals ready to eat"), trail mix, candy, Gatorade and water. But within days, breakfast, lunch and din-ner were trucked in from Houston and served in the make-shift dining area. However, the devastation was so widespread that there was no lodging available for us during the initial stages of the operation. We continued to commute to and from the hotel in north Houston, hoping other arrangements could be made soon.

So during those first two weeks, after a fourteen-hour day, we drove an hour and forty minutes back to our hotel. In the morn-ing, we left Houston around five a.m. to arrive in Beaumont just before dawn. During the dark drive we listened to the one Beaumont radio station that remained on the air. They were broadcasting public service information regarding Red Cross and FEMA locations, as well as anticipated times of food and water distribution at the mall parking lot which had become a tent city for refugees. Progress reports on the utility companies, locations of open businesses, and government announcements were aired interspersed with an occasional song celebrating patriotism, strength and survival. The station also took calls on air from people trying to reunite with family members or folks in need of some service in a town that was, for the most part, closed down. For example, a woman called in saying she had a flat tire thanks to the scattered storm debris that littered the roadways with nails and glass. She hadn't been able to find any place open to repair it. A gentleman caller responded with the name and location of a tire store that was open for business. Beaumont had taken a devastating blow but we were heartened to see the entire community pooling resources.

Our daily commute took us past rows of leaning power poles. Twenty-two of Beaumont's twenty-four power grids were destroyed and had to be rebuilt. When the power was restored to a structure, any wires that had been damaged by the storm short-circuited. Nearly every morning we saw a fire from a burning home. The smoke and fire rose from these homes almost as if they were a sacrifice or burnt offering for the return of some semblance of civilization to a ravaged community. For two weeks we made that arduous trip. Every day I was more drained and Karen was feeling it too. It soon became painfully obvious that we would not be able to sustain the commute.

Fortunately, as progress was made on the infrastructure, more rooms became available in Beaumont. Finally a room was secured for us in the wind- and water-damaged Elegante Hotel. All of the windows in the lobby and some in the guest rooms were boarded up, carpeting and sheetrock had been removed, and on several floors even the walls between the rooms had been removed. The hotel had a generator for power and questionable, brown, running water for bathing. When done with our shower, we would use a jug of distilled water to rinse off. Still, we were grateful not to have the long drive to and from Houston.

With a shorter commute, we were able to get into a routine. In the morning I read the Bible to Karen as she put on her make-up and fixed her hair. She read to me from Max Lucado's <u>Grace for the Moment</u> while I drove us to work, and again in the evenings before we went to sleep. Occasionally, I shared these messages with coworkers and, eventually, I had a small group that would meet with me fifteen minutes before work to discuss the "Word of the Day." This opened the way for several of my coworkers to open their hearts to me about fear and death and life everlasting. We would talk and pray and I would share my F.R.O.G. story of how the Holy Spirit was with me throughout my ordeal with cancer.

During this time, a co-worker slipped up beside my desk and whispered to me, "I'm afraid of dying." Carla went on to say that she had lost both of her parents and recently lost other family and friends to death. I asked her if she was fearful of the actual act of dying or the finality of death. Carla responded, "Both, I suppose. I just can't get it off of my mind."

Carla asked me what I thought about dying. I told her that I fear dying mostly because I don't know when, where and how I will die. Also I don't know—nor do I want to—what pain will accompany the process. I live in the shadow of cancer and the memory of the dreadful pain it brought. Therefore, I am vigilant and respect it. But, like death and dying, I try not to dwell on it because life and my faith are preparing me for the crossing. *"...and might free those who through fear of death were subject to slavery all their lives." Hebrews 2:15*

The next day at work, Carla brought me a stuffed frog holding a rose. It rocks from side to side while singing Louis Armstrong's version of "What a Wonderful World."

During my time in Beaumont, Carla and I had ample opportunity to continue our discussions about overcoming the fear of death. Others at the office confronted me about my brush with mortality and we had many long talks about the fear of facing death. Those discussions forced me to analyze my own feelings on the subject.

Fear of Death

When I first felt compelled to write about death and dying, I had no idea how to address such a seemingly grim topic. Death isn't something one should dwell on and we are rarely prepared for. Several people who were aware I had been at death's door during my battle against cancer have come to me and asked my thoughts on the subject. Is it just morbid curiosity on their part, imagining the Grim Reaper holding his scythe, or a genuine concern? I found that some were so overburdened with worry and the dread of facing the inevitable that the joys of living had been drained from them. I was asked if I thought about dying a lot, how I felt about death, and was I scared. I knew I had to write about death but had no idea how to put it into words. How can I address the drama of death and dying with respect and meaning?

Dying is commonly thought of as the process leading to death, the end of corporeal life. Several writers have commented that we are all dying from the moment we are born, each of us moving inexorably towards that moment when our bodies will cease to harbor breath. But usually when someone says, "I'm dying," they mean that they are close enough to know that the end is relatively near.

When I was much younger, I worked as a death-and-dying counselor in a psychiatric clinic. I had been taught the five stages of grief experienced by the dying which had been outlined by Dr. Elizabeth Kubler-Ross. They are denial, anger, bargaining, depression and acceptance. This is all well and good for counseling the terminally ill, but what do you say to someone who is worried sick about dying when they aren't even sick? There are many who live with this fear daily.

Fear serves a primitive biological purpose in our lives and we wouldn't live long without it. Fear gives us power, triggered by our nervous system to fight or flee from danger. Besides creating a biological imperative to run from a real physical threat, fear can be useful in our lives. In anticipation of an event, fear creates anxiety and restlessness and, in most cases, elicits a response to rectify the situation. It is an inborn response needed for survival and the ability to plan, protect, and thrive. We are often fearful of things that we do not understand, for knowledge is power. Without knowledge, we run from the unknown because instinct tells us it's the right thing to do at the time.

When a fear becomes counterproductive in a person's life, psychologists label it a phobia. Although sometimes used interchangeably, there is a difference between necrophobia, fear of death in general, and thanatophobia, fear of one's own dying. Only a language pundit (no pun intended) could come up with these Greek named phobias. A phobia is a mind killer: it steals pleasure, hopes, and dreams and replaces them with dark thoughts.

Death and dying are surrounded with uncertainty. For me, fear of dying reflects the trepidation regarding the actual process of shedding this mortal coil...pain, suffering, losing control, lingering. Whereas fear of death reflects the uncertainty of what occurs after the actual moment of death. All of us, to some extent, fear one or the other or both. Will I be able to bear what I will endure during the process of dying? Is there an afterlife or will I find myself in oblivion with all of life's knowledge in one hand, experiences in the other and carrying my soul over my shoulder?

Anticipation of this unavoidable event can create anxiety and lead to fear. We all know that we will die *someday*. How do we handle that prospect in our daily lives? How do we face the possibility that we could die suddenly, today or tomorrow? How do we handle the process of dying if we are given a prognosis that gives us not a sudden death but one that will occur in weeks, months, years?

The answer is in how we prepare for death and the way we surrender to it. And that, in part, depends on our spiritual beliefs regarding what happens to us after we die. We approach death with ease or fear depending on what we have learned. I believe that death requires an enormous amount of preparation...a lifetime, in fact. For I know that death is a new beginning, our last earthly step before opening our eyes in the presence of God.

Death and dying may be beyond our control, but that doesn't mean we are powerless over the process. When death demands our life's resume, it should include moral and spiritual details about how we prepared for this moment. Death's door is no place to attempt to slapdash your affairs in order. Just like preparing a will or medical power of attorney, preparing for death spiritually and mentally can provide solace while dying and change our perspective and, hopefully, that of others while we are yet living. The only way to have power over death and dying is to prepare for it and, believe me, you and your loved ones will be grateful. Being alive to the fact that we will die inspires us to live wisely, appreciate life and allows us to die without fear or regret.

I met a man who told me he was an atheist and said, "When you're dead, you're gone." Jake went on to say there is no God, no Supreme Being, no life after death. Somewhat troubled, I asked him what he thought about my belief in God. Without hesitation Jake said, "I respect your beliefs and would expect you to honor mine." Jake told me that several years ago he had a major heart attack and the paramedics were able to revive him. Jake said that at age 63 he was getting old and would have rather died and moved on to make room for someone else.

Later I thought, "How sad and lonely this man must be." I wondered how he would fill the spiritual void in his soul in preparation for his life's end. As God's disciple, I felt as if I had let both my heavenly Father and my brother, Jake, down. Bewildered, I wondered how I could have spread the gospel to a man who would hear yet not listen. Is Jake really true to himself, not afraid and did not judge others? It came to me too late; all I had to do is use four words, "What if you're wrong?"

Seven years prior to my ordeal I had lost my eldest brother, Jeff, to lung and brain cancer on Christmas morning. As I began writing this, Jeff's two daughters were caring for their mother who was also terminally ill with cancer. My brother's wife, Dolder, called her two daughters to her bedside and apologized for smoking all those years and asked for their forgiveness. She told them she thought that she could get away with smoking even though that's what probably took her husband, Jeff. Don't smoke, and if you do, quit! Not all diseases are self-inflicted, and cancer certainly isn't one of them, for it doesn't discriminate. There are lots of people who die of cancer who don't smoke or drink, but why tempt fate.

Jeff had lived nine months from the diagnosis of cancer to that early Christmas morning. He hadn't handled the process of dying very well. He expressed a great deal of anger in the form of shouting and cursing at his loved ones. And he didn't turn to God until his last moments.

His two daughters, Debbie and Monika, sneaked into their father's hospital room early that Christmas morning. Their father had been in a coma for over two months and had but hours to live. They came bearing presents to say their goodbyes. Debbie had my brother's cat – yes, a real, live kitty…in a bag and her sister had several posters of James Dean and my brother's other hero, Bob Dylan. Debbie took my brother's cat out of the bag – literally…and placed it under my brother's limp hand while Monika unfurled the posters in front of her comatose father.

It was Christmas morning in Fort Walton Beach, Florida and the family was together to celebrate the Lord's birthday and the celebration of life. While my brother's daughters were talking to their mother, they noticed their daddy's hand gently petting his cat. Jeff opened his eyes and asked his family to come to his bedside to pray with him. After the prayer and while he was petting his kitty, the girls noticed it was starting to snow. A real fairy tale story. SNOW in Florida on Christmas morning. The flakes were brilliant white and the size of quarters, melting as they touched the ground. Excited, the girls said, "Look, Daddy, it's snowing!" as they pushed his bed closer to the window for a better view. My brother looked out of the window towards heaven and back at his family. Then, still clutching his cat, he closed his eyes.

Later on, Sister Grace, a family friend who was a Catholic nun for over sixty years, told me if you died on Christmas, you go straight to Heaven---I believe her.

Jeff had a deathbed conversion; that is, he wished to follow the tenets of his belief at the very last moment. However, Jeff was not prepared for death, which caused great anguish, frustration and sadness in him and others until his acceptance. His wife, Dolder, walked with him to death's door while she and their children and grandchildren endured his yelling, cursing and screaming all the way till his final hours.

On the other hand, Dolder's dying was filled with her love for Christ and others. She lifted our spirits and had a smile as though she was looking at the face of Jesus. Just prior to her death, she told me, "Michael, God is not through with me yet." How can two people sentenced to death by cancer go through the process, one with sovereign power over death while the other becomes spiritually and morally repugnant in the face of death? Planning and preparation for dying is imperative, not just for ourselves. The way we approach, and ultimately accept, death will affect our loved ones who follow.

Finding satisfaction in life depends on how you spend that precious time allotted you. If you squander that gift, before you know it, life may pass you by. Time well spent can be more valuable than diamonds, sapphires, rubies or emeralds. So how does one use the hourglass to live life to its fullest? It's easier if you know how much sand is left. But what if you don't? First, find life's purpose and create order from the chaos. Dreams are messages from our subconscious mind and our future is not predestined. If you set your mind to something, you may be able to do more in an hour than some can do in a day, week, month or even a lifetime.

Dolder used her remaining time wisely by spending it with God, her children and grandchildren. She even found time to work in her garden, pray and study the word of God before He called her home. My brother, Jeff, addressed the value of time in a commentary on mankind (quoted later in this book). Hold your minutes, hours, and days close to your heart for we do not know when life will shatter our hourglass and spill the unlived sands of time. Hold on tight to your dreams for they hold the key to tomorrow.

How do I feel about death and dying? Like most, I struggle with the prospect, but the way I deal with it is to constantly ask Jesus to cleanse the sins from my soul. I have a living will drawn up by my attorney to instruct my family about the way I want the physical and legal aspects of my dying to be handled. But I also have a dying will drawn up by my spirit to instruct me about the way I want to handle the spiritual and emotional aspects of my dying. Since I've been there once, there have been several revisions. I find that with sin I am troubled, with prayer I am comforted and death I fear not. Only through Christ can I walk safely and fear no evil. The devil tries to get me to be fearful; but as a Christian, I trust in the Lord Christ Jesus and accept him as my Savior. I believe the Holy Spirit has instructed me to put this to word and in doing so, I praise our heavenly Father and place my trust in God and not fear. *"In righteousness you will be established; You will be far from oppression, for you will not fear; And from terror, for it will not come near you."* Isaiah 54:14 I pray that some will find solace in these words...Amen.

***

My time in Beaumont gave me opportunities to discuss spiritual matters with my coworkers other than the fear of dying. Karen had given me a small stuffed frog to put on my computer at work since I kept Rad in our hotel room. Every week or so some soul who had begun to Fully Rely On God would place a small stuffed frog, book or picture of a frog on my desk. The frogs started to multiply around my desk and computer. As the weeks went by, the frog congregation drew the curious from other work groups who inquired about the meaning and, thereby, even more people were told the meaning of F.R.O.G. I had prayed before we left Jackson for God to send me where he could use me. I knew that God had sent me to the right place at the right time to spread His word. He brought me to His divine appointments on an almost daily basis.

One of the copiers broke down at the office, so I called the 800 number to who-knows-where to request repair service. While taking my report, the woman who answered the phone said, out of the blue, "It takes a real special person to do what you do, going around the country helping people whose homes have been damaged or destroyed. My prayers are with you."

I told her, "My wife is full time with the company. Since I retired I've followed her around the country working as a temporary employee."

She replied, "Then you are both special and my prayers are with both of you."

Warming up to the sincerity in her voice, I continued, "I have a stuffed frog sitting on my computer. You should get one for yours. F.R.O.G. stands for Fully Rely On God. Every time I look at it, I'm reminded that the Holy Spirit is always with me and to pray."

This kind stranger replied, "I'm writing that down. I'm always listening for messages from God. I think I just heard one and I really needed one today."

On another occasion one of the adjusters approached my desk and told me he wanted to quit smoking. He had spoken to me before. Having asked the standard, "What's with all the frogs," he had been told the meaning behind F.R.O.G. Now he was coming to me for help or hope with this habit that he wanted to overcome out of his love for his daughters. I don't know what he was expecting, but at an inner prompting I invoked the Holy Spirit and began to pray over him. Occasionally, at times like these I am drawn deeply into the presence of the Holy Spirit and am not always totally aware of my surroundings. I vaguely remember praying with him to the Holy Spirit about his addiction. I envisioned a scenario of his two daughters growing up fatherless and, before I knew it, this man was on his knees, weeping at my desk in the presence of over a hundred people looking up from their tables in the office. To this day I have no idea what I said to evoke this kind of response. A short time later he was released from that assignment. I have no way of knowing if he was able to quit smoking, but I pray that he did.

Impatience

On the way to work one morning, I reminded Karen that we needed to go by the pharmacy to refill one of my prescriptions. We stopped at Walgreen's only to be told that, since it was a controlled substance and we were from "out of state," I would need to see a doctor to have a new prescription written. Pointing to the five refills indicated on the bottle, I informed the pharmacist that their drugstore chain advertises they can refill your prescriptions anywhere in the United States. To which he replied, "Yep, all except Texas."

Feeling my frustration level rise, I retorted, "I'll just have my doctor call in a new prescription!"

"He can," the pharmacist responded, "if he resides in the state of Texas."

Thwarted in our mission by the vagaries of state law, we left in a huff in search of the nearest walk-in clinic. As we were leaving, I wondered how something so simple could become so complicated.

I called the office to let them know that I needed some time off to see a doctor to have my prescription refilled. The secretary, who was from Beaumont, directed us to a clinic that was giving priority to disaster relief victims and relief personnel. It wasn't far from the office so I figured we could slip in, pick up the prescription, go back to the pharmacy and return to work. As it turned out, it wasn't going to be that easy. It never is.

We located the clinic and made our way through the entrance into a mammoth waiting area. There were chairs all around the room and some in the middle. I didn't count them, even though I had plenty of time to do so. As we made our way towards the reception desk, I looked around and counted about a dozen patients and thought, 'Even if I have to wait, this shouldn't take that long.' In fact the earth's tectonic plates move faster during continental drift than the one physician on call that day.

I checked in with the receptionist and explained that all I needed was a Texas prescription for a drug for which I already had five refills in Arizona. She promptly handed me the all-too-familiar clip-board with personal information and medical history forms to fill out and said, "It'll be ninety-six dollars – up front– to see the doctor."

I explained that I was in town temporarily with the disaster relief people and reiterated, "All I need is a refill for my medication."

With a stone cold gaze, she told me, "We accept cash, a personal check with identification or a major credit card."

I pleaded, "Do I really have to see a doctor?" The stone wall was unmovable.

Karen paid the fee and we retreated to our chairs in the waiting room. I returned the completed form to the receptionist and asked, "How long do I have to wait?"

Without glancing up she replied, "The nurse will call you."

The Lord wants me to learn patience during this second life he granted me. I know this because he never misses an opportunity to teach me when I demonstrate that I'm not doing a very good job at it. An hour passed, then two. I turned to Karen and told her that we should have just driven across the Texas border and had the prescription filled in Louisiana but, alas, by this time we had too much time and money invested in this debacle. My youth was vanishing before my eyes as I grew older with anger and the burning torment of impatience. I felt no contrition or remorse as my impatience turned to exasperation. I approached the receptionist and again my pleas fell on deaf ears. I turned around to return to my seat and noticed that the waiting area was almost full. I mused dolefully that some of these people might not live long enough to see the doctor.

I could no longer contain my impatience, so I began pacing back and forth like an obnoxious, overanxious child in front of the reception desk. I stomped and huffed and sighed and muttered under my breath. After about thirty minutes, I noticed that the waiting area was almost empty again. I had watched as some were called back to see the phantom doctor, while others who had given up departed to find another clinic or went home to expire. If I was in line to go to hell, which I was, I would have not been so anxious.

Figuring that I had nothing to lose, I once again approached the ice queen to inquire about my status. In hopes of breaking through her seeming indifference, I played the Cancer Card: "I've been battling cancer for the past nine months and I really need that prescription."

At that, she held up her right forearm, defiantly displaying her pink wrist band below her clenched fist. She stated with obvious irritation, "I'm currently battling breast cancer and THIS JOB, too."

She left to go in back to talk to the doctor and see if he could see me next. She left me thinking, "Wow! What have I done? This woman is a fellow survivor just trying to make it through another day. And I, in my fit of self-pity, impatience, and indignation, have just made her job that much harder."

Almost immediately, I was ushered back to an examination room and figured that I was escorted there to either starve to death or die. The doctor promptly appeared and I, unchastened by my moments-old insight, unloaded my wrath on him. I know that a doctor signature can be illegible, but I believe the scribble on the prescription I was holding in my hand was induced by the speed with which it was written. The doctor confided that he was only allowed to prescribe five days of this medication, but because of the circumstances, he had written the prescription for thirty days. I think he wanted to get rid of me and I don't blame him.

Believe me, what you have just read is a mild version of the true story of how I behaved. I didn't want to write this, nor share it, nor experience it again through writing it. To this day I am still ashamed of the way I acted and how I treated others. The reason I told this story is not to lessen my culpability for my transgression, for I have been absolved by God. I shared this because I am spiritually and morally weak. As children of our Lord, we will stumble and fall. *"Keep watching and praying that you may not enter into temptation; the spirit is willing, but the flesh is weak." Matthew 26:41* Satan loves this part of my life because he believes he can hold it over my head. I will not afford him the opportunity to do that.

Patience

I'm not going to give you the definition, for we all know what patience isn't. I realize the Lord wants me to learn patience during my second life on earth, maybe as a penance for the first.

Did you know that God has a traffic light in Beaumont, Texas with my name on it? That's right, for nearly six months I stopped at that light four times a day on the way to and fro and during lunch while working Hurricane Rita. After weeks of observation, we determined that the light was not triggered by traffic on the tiny side street it served. We would sit through the red light while nothing passed in either direction. We also determined that the light wasn't on any sort of timer. We could see it from the parking lot at work. It would be green for an hour only to turn red when we were in our car headed towards it.

As we approached my red light, Karen and I would turn towards each other with bated breath, and I don't mean chewing on worms. We eventually got to the point where we would laugh hysterically when the light turned red as we approached it, although sometimes I grumbled. I roughly calculated that we spent over five hours at our red light. When you ask the Lord to give you patience, He doesn't give it to you; He teaches it to you one red light at a time. The secret to learning patience is not merely being passive or tolerant, but to find something worthwhile to do in the meantime. The house on the corner at my red light had a lovely garden and I learned to enjoy watching it unfold with the turning season.

Most of us are impatient which results in selfishness, grief and loss of temper. Like ironing, patience can smooth life's wrinkles with spiritual calmness, self control and a leap of faith. I don't know why I have procrastinated adding patience to life's "to-do" list. If I would have only learned it sooner, I would have become more even-tempered and less likely to be irritated by instigators. The one thing I struggle with daily is patience. To accept provocation, annoyance, pain, and misfortune and to persevere with courage in trying circumstances is unrelenting patience. Boy, do I have a long way to go! Lord, give me patience and please hurry. I need it A.S.A.P.

What then is the best way to learn to live a life of patience? The gospels have taught me that Jesus was the epitome of patience and the Bible addresses patience in scripture more than I ever imagined. It's difficult to be patient when your problems seem insurmountable and people are unchangeable. *"So, as those who have been chosen of God, holy and beloved, put on a heart of compassion, kindness, humility, gentleness and patience; bearing with one another, and forgiving each other, whoever has a complaint against anyone; just as the Lord forgave you, so also should you."* Colossians 3:12-13

Helen Keller said, "We could never learn to be brave and patient if there were only joy in the world." Without trials and tribulations, we could never learn patience. But once learned, patience allows most of life's challenges to fall into place and tempers life's journey with sufferance and perseverance, so we can bear affliction without complaint. John Quincy Adams said, "Patience and perseverance have a magical effect before which difficulties disappear and obstacles vanish."

Why do most want to be on a bullet-train through life rather than on a leisurely stroll? There is much to learn before we go before the Lord and present Him with our praises, gifts, talents, and earthly lessons learned. That's why we're here. If we knew it all and there was no learning to take place, we would have been born in heaven. Life seems to start on a dirt road, but soon we turn onto a street then enter the highway and before we know it, we're on the freeways and expressways of life. By the way, that noise you heard overhead was grandma's jet; she's catching up with the others on the overnight express. At breakneck speeds we cannot smell the roses, much less attempt to pick one. I thought mother's milk was 'fast food,' but that too has been replaced with microwaveable dinners and MRE's. Patience is not about high speed internet, Jiffy Lube, microwave popcorn or the "ME" generation. What's next, fast faith or road rage on the highway to hell?

Patience is endurance, steadfast and unable to be rushed. *"He who is slow to anger has great understanding, But he who is quick-tempered exalts folly." Proverbs 14:29.*

Why do we need patience? Because everything we do in life requires it—long lines of people in the emergency room, life and death, traffic or being placed on hold indefinitely. What are the rewards of patience? There are various degrees of patience. One example would be a child waiting for dad to come home from work so they can pick up the new puppy. Another would be someone behind you blowing their horn seconds after the light turns green…that takes the definition to another level. There are times when you wait patiently for naught like a promotion, a loan to buy your first home, or a favorable PET scan after completing cancer treatment. As we learn patience, the rewards of composure outweigh the distress of restlessness when confronted with delay.

What are the consequences of impatience? I believe the opposite of patience is evil, which can deceive, causing meanness, hatred, anger, rage. It can lead to mayhem or even murder. When we lose our patience, we become upset not only at others but also ourselves. The "ME" generation throws away relationships, people, jobs – anything that doesn't work out the way they want it to and as quickly as they want it to. Why do we allow impatience to deplete the very thing most needed? We're wasting spiritual energy turning away others who support us because they are slow and don't see it our way.

Impatience sacrifices friendships and relationships because they don't agree with you and you are unable to thoroughly change them as quickly as you desire. Impatience looks at the negative and ignores the positive and is pessimistic rather than optimistic about life. Stop being angry and so hard on yourself and others, for all we need is 'a little bit of patience.' Don't stifle the ones you love with negativity or by being demanding, blaming and pessimistic in an attempt to bring them beneath you. When you are impatient, do you feel frustrated, anxious, tense, stressed or ill-tempered? Remember, impatience is about you; patience is about others.

Patience will trump impatience by acknowledging that each day is a gift from the Lord. Above all, accept your own imperfections, weaknesses and faults. Love yourself first, become your own best friend and accept others that are struggling with life's crises and setbacks. Let go and let God and realize that all anxieties and worries are not to be blamed on others. According to a Dutch proverb, "A handful of patience is worth more than a bushel of brains." Patience is like 'Catch 22.' Stanislaw J. Lec said, "You must first have a lot of patience to learn to have patience." The Lord's discipline is patience, and he who has it cannot hold it but dispenses it to others through practice. As you read this, I ask for your patience because, "God is not finished with me yet."

Lee Ann Le Picard
[b. March 17, 1957 d. April 12, 2006]

While I was working on computer files, a man named Glen paused at my desk on his way to the mail basket and asked,

"What's up with the frogs?" I responded, "I thought you'd never ask." Then I told him how I had learned to Fully Rely On God during my battle with cancer.

Glen's a likable guy, an outgoing, hard-working claims adjuster at the office in Beaumont, Texas. Cancer has been a major villain in his life as it took both of his parents. We talked about faith and he told me that he had struggled with it since he had no religious upbringing. He had gone searching on his own spiritual path and had settled on Christianity.

Several weeks later Glen came to my desk with a Gideon's Bible he had retrieved from the nightstand at the hotel. Although Glen was familiar with how the Gideon's Bible came to be in his room, now, much to his surprise, he knows *why* it was there. Glen wanted to know if I had any suggested reading. It seems the genealogies of the early chapters left him tongue-tied. As a beginner, I suggested he start with the books of the New Testament, the gospels according to Matthew, Mark, Luke and John. Having received the direction he was seeking, he took off like a shot, smiling and clasping his Bible. Every few days Glen would stop in and talk with me about his Bible study and walk in faith with the Lord. Spirit-filled souls have a glow or aura around them which can be mistaken for nothing else. Glen truly glowed.

What father could refuse to forgive his child who looks up at him and says, "I am sorry, Father, for what I have done. Please forgive me." "…*to open their eyes so that they may turn from darkness to light and from the dominion of Satan to God, that they may receive forgiveness of sins and an inheritance among those who have been sanctified by faith in Me." Acts 26:18*

Early one March morning, Glen approached my desk and could barely get the words out. "My sister, Lee Ann, was just diagnosed with cancer. She's in the hospital in Pensacola and they're trying to find out where she *doesn't* have cancer." The very word *cancer* brings to mind a pernicious neoplasm that spreads mayhem, death, and destruction throughout the body and tears at one's soul.

I reached out to my brother and held him tight as I spoke. "You need to go see her. Lee Ann needs you to be with her to pray with her and pray over her." *"Is anyone among you sick? Then he must call for the elders of the church and they are to pray over him, anointing him with oil in the name of the Lord." James 5:14*

Glen responded, "I have a weekend off coming up. I'll be visiting her very soon."

Just a day before that weekend approached, he came to me again and said he was just too busy to leave. "I can't go this week. I've got too much work to do. I can wait a couple of weeks and go then."

Holding onto him, I shook him and said, "NO! You must go now." He obviously didn't fathom the urgency of Lee Ann's grave and impending life-and-death struggle...I knew.

At the time, Glen was working for my wife, Karen, so I asked him to come with me to her desk. She was aware of his sister's condition and knew he was scheduled to be off the next weekend so he could go visit her. I blurted out to her that Glen felt that he couldn't go. She turned to Glen and asked, "Why can't you go?" Glen explained that he had stacks of files assigned to him that required payments and appointments for inspections. He didn't want any of his customers to have to wait. Karen told him to bring her all of his files that needed attention before his return from his weekend with his sister. She assured him that his files would be taken care of and that none of the customers would be inconvenienced, so he could visit his sister as planned. She then proceeded to have a very intimate and persuasive conversation with him. I returned to my desk with a sense of deep relief.

That day during our lunch hour, Karen and I searched for the elusive perfect frog in a town still recovering from Hurricane Rita. Due to time constraints, we had to adopt the first one that hopped along. There was a gift shop near the place where we ate lunch and figured it would be a good place to hunt. While we were shopping, I noticed the salesclerk arranging figurines. She accidently nudged one and it began to fall, but she nimbly caught it before it hit the floor.

"Nice snag," I commented.

She just smiled and said, "Can I help you find something."

"I'm looking for Easter frogs. I see bunnies, chicks and ducks, but no frogs."

She didn't look at me like I was nuts; she just started showing me frogs. Not Easter frogs…just frogs, but with each she gave a suggestion for ribbon or some other trim to make it an Easter frog. I told her the meaning of frog and that I was looking for a special one for a friend whose sister had cancer.

"Oh, I do know the meaning of F.R.O.G." she said. "I don't worry about much 'cause I figure He's taken care of me so far; why would I think He'd stop now?" She went on to confide, "I had breast cancer. Nothing as terrible as some poor folks, I'm really lucky." Then she took off her glasses giggling. "I wear a wig and it makes it tough on the glasses. They're either under the wig or on top where they get all lopsided. I haven't had a chance to get my new contacts yet. It's just a little thing. I figure I'll let God have the big things and I'll take the little things. He gave me the ability to take care of those for myself."

We settled for a small, not too homely, ceramic frog perched on a ball. (In case you're wondering, the sentimental value of the frog gift becomes inseparable from symbolic meaning when the frog is presented with the F.R.O.G. story. That said you may understand how an inanimate object transcends frog to become F.R.O.G.)

Karen worked with Glen to redistribute his files and he was ready to leave the next day. When Glen returned to the office with bags packed, I presented him with this porcelain frog to bring to his sister. I told him to tell her this is but a reminder to pray to the Holy Spirit who is always with her and to Fully Rely On God. *"But when He, the Spirit of truth, comes, He will guide you into all the truth; for He will not speak on His own initiative, but whatever He hears, He will speak; and He will disclose to you what is to come." John 16:13*

The following Monday Glen came into the office with a big grin and proceeded to tell me about his visit. When he had arrived, Lee Ann was still heavily sedated, had very little strength, and tired easily. The next morning she was more alert and they shared stories about their youth. He told of how they played hide-and-go-seek, and I could imagine him covering his eyes as a child would have done while playing the game. They both ran away from home one afternoon but returned before it got dark because they were scared. He said, "We laughed and joked while talking about our childhood, reliving cherished memories." He went on to tell of how they had little arguments and ketchup fights as children and how they grew closer as adults.

As they were reminiscing about the past, Glen remembered the frog I had given him to bring to Lee Ann. As he presented her with the gift, he told her the story of the Holy Spirit and the power of prayer and the meaning of F.R.O.G. Excited, she asked her brother to place the frog on top of the armoire opposite the foot of her bed so she could look up and see it and it would remind her to pray. As Glen walked across the room toward the armoire, he had to pass the window. He glanced out the window and saw a REAL FROG clinging to the outside of the screen. According to Glen, the frog had one hand stretched up as if pointing towards heaven and was peering at them over his lower hand and shoulder. Glen said he got goose bumps and his hand began to tremble so much that he was afraid he would drop Lee Ann's ceramic frog as he put it in place.

As he prepared to leave, Glen asked his sister if he could get her anything else. "Yes," she replied, "I would love to have a strawberry sundae." Glen went out and brought back the desired treat. Then, as the day drew to a close, Lee Ann enjoyed as much of her prize as her frail body could handle. Glen said it was a wonderful day and such a blessing to share that time with his beloved sister. "I'm so glad I went!"

Two days later, early on Wednesday morning, Glen came into the office, walked up to me with a smile, and grabbed me in a powerful bear hug. "Every day is a gift from the Lord," he affirmed.

I responded, "Indeed it is."

Still smiling, Glen said, "The Lord took my sister at 2:15 this morning," and after hugs, tears and blessings, he headed for his desk.

That time – 2:15 a.m. – was significant. When I was lying in a semi-comatose state expecting to die, the Holy Spirit grabbed hold of me, pulled me from my bed and to my feet saying, "I have work for you to do." I had glanced at the clock. It was 2:15 a.m. That time had been embedded in my memory for six months, and with Glen's pronouncement, it suddenly took on greater significance. I am now kind of a "Ghost Writer" for the Holy Ghost and I will spread the gospel and do His bidding as called upon.

***

Two years to the day later I had a chance meeting with Glen in Fort Worth, Texas. I told him I had written this story about him and his sister Lee Ann and requested his permission to include it in this book. I printed a draft copy and asked him to prayerfully consider it. The next day, Glen returned the draft and asked, "How did you remember every word I told you?" He said he had cried when he read it and hadn't remembered that he told me in such detail what transpired. He had placed a little yellow sticky at the top of the first page with Lee Ann's date of birth and the date of her rebirth with God. Glen asked if I would add "although Glen was familiar with how the Gideon's Bible came to be in his room; now, to his surprise, he knows why it was there."

***

I believe the Lord orchestrates…that is, He arranges opportunities for our choice. Two of His sheep came home. They were never lost for He knew where they were.

With every FROG encounter, I see that God has a plan and sends me where I can fulfill this purpose. The following day, Glen presented me with a rather homely ceramic frog perched on a globe with a mouse pad in substitute for a lily pad to place his gift on. The lily/mouse pad had a beach scene with palm trees. I smile every time I see it, for I know how powerful and loving our Lord is and I pray.

Shortly after this, we were given a departure date from Beaumont. There was still much more work to do but fewer people would be needed on-site to do it. Since we had been out on assignment for six months and had a scheduled vacation coming up, it made sense that we would be the next to leave.

The folks we worked with threw a going-away party for us, with all kinds of wonderful food and a cake fashioned of individual cupcakes in the shape of a google-eyed frog. There were also "lovely parting gifts" featuring frogs in various capacities. It was hard to say goodbye. We were leaving behind coworkers who had become friends. But we knew that God's timing is perfect. He would have other work for us down the road, more people in need of a FROG.

***

ANDRE

Andre is a big, muscular black man with an infectious smile and an inner spirituality like sunshine. We had worked together before but met again in Kansas City, Kansas. One of the great joys Karen and I experienced while working around the country was meeting wonderful, genuine people. The joy was redoubled when we would reconnect with them months or years later. We were both glad to see Andre again because we love his ebullient spirit. But Kansas City was a short assignment of only four weeks, so our reunion was brief.

As Karen and I were preparing to leave, I was distributing frogs to those people in the office with whom I had formed a spiritual bond. Andre was chatting with some friends when he saw me headed his way with the fuzzy green offering. "Oh, my gosh!" he exclaimed. "I'm getting a frog. I'M GETTING A FROG! Do you know what that means? F.R.O.G. – Fully Rely On God. That's so cool!"

I told Andre to take his frog everywhere he goes, and every time he sees it to remember to pray. He assured me that his frog would ride with him in his van to all his job sites.

A year and a half later, I met up with Andre again in San Diego while he was working claims from the wildfires. Andre confided in me that he and his wife had been having problems with their relationship when he was in Kansas. They seemed to be fighting a lot. But he showed her his frog I had given him and told her what it meant. He said their problems all seemed to vanish after he brought F.R.O.G. home. It reminded him to pray and pray he did.

Some of God's children carry Bibles, rosaries, or medallions of Saints. Others wear a crucifix around their neck or a devotional pendant and a religious bracelet as reminders to pray and worship. We're here to know, love and serve God Almighty, and for me, F.R.O.G. is but another reminder to pray and give thanks.

SUSIE

The last time I had been at the Cancer Treatment Center was for a three-month check-up. I remember the two receptionists laughing and high-fiving as I came through the door carrying Rad. When I asked them what that was all about, Jan replied they had a lunch bet as to whether or not I'd show up with my stuffed frog. When I asked who won, Jan reached to retrieve her stuffed kitty, Inky, from her computer monitor. Smiling, she shook Inky in a celebratory dance and said, "I did."

Now that I had returned home from the long assignment in Beaumont, Rad and I stopped at the Cancer Center in hopes of catching up with the social worker, Cathy. I wanted to personally thank her for the tremendous amount of support and encouragement she gave me while I was a patient there. The receptionist said, "I'm sorry. Cathy's out of the office attending a class. She'll be gone for the next two weeks." She paused thoughtfully and then mentioned, "There's a support group meeting Friday at noon. Do you think your frog, Rad, could attend?"

I told her, "If Rad comes, I'll have to come too because he can't drive. He doesn't have a license and his legs are so short they don't reach the pedals." She grinned as she wrote the date and time on a sticky note and placed it on Rad's shirt.

Friday we arrived for the meeting and were directed to a small conference room. Not knowing what to expect, I placed Rad on an end table behind me so he wouldn't distract anyone. Then I took a seat across from the therapist, hoping that would keep me out of trouble. Soon the other survivors arrived. It appeared they all knew one another as they exchanged greetings. Most cancer survivors have some things in common: we've been through hell on earth, and some of us are engaged in a battle we've been told we can't win. Although every person's experience with cancer is different, I believe that only a cancer survivor can truly understand the emotional, psychological and physical struggle that occurs within another cancer patient. To this day, I live a transitory life in the shadow of cancer.

Not all cancer survivors are on the same path but we are all walking in the same forest. In a cancer support group, the people discover they encounter different challenges, depending on the types of cancer they have. Some will cross paths with others fighting the same demon they have encountered such as breast, ovarian, testicular, pancreatic, cervical, and colon cancer. Or they may find themselves on a lonesome road with leukemia, lymphoma, or neck, liver or other less common types of cancer. Although you might not know what monsters are waiting to leap out at you from the gloominess, you can call out to those ahead of you on the trails.

Seven of us were gathered in the conference room, along with a social worker as if we were gathered in a clearing in the forest. We called our names out to one another so we could be recognized. While patiently waiting for the silence to be broken, I gazed about the room and noticed a woman in an ankle cast, a young man wearing medical clogs, an older couple, a gentleman in his mid-seventies whom I recognized from my church, and a nice-looking woman about my age.

"Hey! What happened to your ankle?"

"Oh, I slipped on the ice in the parking lot after last week's chemo treatment."

"That kind of adds injury to insult, doesn't it?"

"Not really. It was what someone said to me after I fell that really hurt."

"What was that?"

"A woman noticed me leaving oncology, and I think that having no hair gave it away that I had cancer. She also witnessed my fall on the ice."

"What did she say?"

"Something to the effect that I must have been really bad in my life to deserve the wrath of God." While trying to hold back her tears, she asked how people could be so cruel.

Ray, the elderly man from my church said, "Apparently that woman is delusional if she doesn't know that bad things can happen to good people." He went on to say that some people are so scared of the "C word" that they associate it with evil. The woman replied, "I realize that, and I pray that woman never has cancer."

Until cancer, I never realized the strong compassionate desire of family, friends and even strangers to alleviate my suffering and soothe my mind with a stroke of a hand and a benevolent whisper for God's mercy. It was a shame that it took cancer for me to see something that beautiful has always been there whether I needed it or not.

The therapist seemed somewhat removed as we went about our discussions dealing with cancer and the side-effects from treatment and the disease itself. The older couple wanted to know how to deal with incessant diarrhea that the husband is experiencing after having most of his colon removed. I replied, "Lomotil! If they would have had that on the Titanic, it would have sucked up all the water and she wouldn't have gone down." There was another request about how to treat radiation burns and nausea. "Bag Balm for the burns," I quickly responded. "It's a petrolatum-lanolin-based ointment that farmers have been using on their cows' udders and their hands for over a hundred years. As for nausea, rubbing in circles on top of your big toes and cheek bones won't stop the locomotive but will slow it down to where you can board it." The last two remedies were told to me by someone that was ahead of me on the path through the forest. After a few chuckles, the discussion turned to a more serious note.

The young man wearing the medical clogs was an RN in the final stage of leukemia. He was upbeat as he shared his experiences as a nurse. He was confident he was a good one. He went on to confide that after becoming a patient, he became an even better nurse and a formidable teacher in the field of nursing. It is said that medical personnel make the worst patients, but from what I know of this man, he was outstanding at both nursing and dealing with his own afflictions. His skills in humanity and nursing were beyond reproach. Without the human factor, like the God factor, there is a gaping wound that will never heal. If you just try to heal the body but refrain from tending the human frailty, you will fail. Today, God is surely smiling upon this man who taught us so much in his brief remaining time. And through us, he will continue to teach others that we meet on the path of our lives.

Ray was aware of my struggle against squamous cell esophageal cancer during the past year, as was most of my church family. Ray stood up and addressed the woman who was about my age, sitting on a sofa to my left. Pointing to me he said, "Susie, Michael has been battling the same type of cancer as you and is a few steps ahead of you in his recovery."

Susie had been struggling down her path alone with blinders on because of the rarity of the disease (less than five percent of all cancers); even her oncologists were unable to provide her with any answers about the relationship between the treatments and her symptoms. Sometimes a doctor may be vague for a reason; but when I ask my physician, trained in the practice of oncology, a question, I don't expect a flippant or ambiguous answer.

Susie jumped to her feet with tears in her eyes; she said, "You are the answer to my prayers."

As I reached for her, I said, "Follow me, for the Lord is leading." We held each others' head and shoulders in our arms, for now we both had someone to relate to and share our fear tears.

After the group session concluded, Susie had a dozen questions. "When will the burning in my throat go away? Will I get my saliva glands back or do I have to carry this bottle of water around with me for the rest of my life? Will my taste-buds come back or will food always taste like I'm chewing on dry cardboard? Do you have problems swallowing; are the sores in your mouth gone?" I responded to her questions with the answers I received from Father Time through the power of the Holy Spirit. Regarding her saliva glands, I told her that I prayed for their return with every sip of water for twenty-four hours and left it in the hands of God. I introduced Susie to Rad, my frog, and invited her to the house to meet my wife, Karen. She accepted the invitation, then told me that she had over one hundred stuffed frogs but never heard anyone refer to F.R.O.G. as "Fully Rely On God."

Karen and I got up early Saturday morning, excited with Susie's pending visit; we wanted to make sure the house was clean and that we had the perfect frog to present to her along with a book by Lynn Eib entitled <u>When God and Cancer Meet</u>. Like faith, no two frogs are the same, and it doesn't matter what foot you start with as long as you move forward. Susie finally arrived and Karen immediately took her in like long-lost family. We presented her with our gifts and we shared stories about our families. I continued with the 'lessons learned' training we began after yesterday's meeting. I told her that she must force herself to eat different foods no matter how bad it might taste or burn. Your taste buds are in training like a baby's, and you must learn to like chicken again. We were already like family as Susie began to leave. "Drive carefully." "Make sure you give us a call." "Let us know if you need anything." "Know that you are in our prayers."

During a phone conversation the following week, Susie told me that after leaving our place last Saturday, she felt a strong urge to find a church and pray. With family problems and her plight with cancer, she had become somewhat removed from her faith.

She said that she drove all over town in search of any church, temple or sanctuary but found them all locked and vacant. Finally, she found solace outside a church that was locked, but inside the organist was practicing for Sunday's service. Standing outside the window, she could see and hear him play as she stood in tearful prayer. This image of my sister finding refuge with God on the lawn outside the church brought me to my knees. I asked her if she would be able to attend services with us on Sunday and she agreed.

I knew Susie was looking for a church family and I was eager to introduce her to ours. Cancer had carved a hole in me; God had filled it. I pray my sister can find a similar relationship. She arrived several minutes before the service started, so there was time for introductions. Her friend, Ray, from the support group arrived and greeted her like a daughter with a big hug and a smile. I had recently asked several of our family members to pray for her complete recovery and for an all-clear on her upcoming PET scan in six weeks. I think she was surprised that so many seemingly knew her and were praying for her. After all, isn't that what a family is all about?

After the service, I and several cancer survivors invited Susie to attend the "Relay for Life." The relay would take place inside our church sanctuary the following Friday, starting at 6 p.m. and ending the next morning at dawn. High school students from all over the area would be walking all night to raise funds through sponsors and donations. The proceeds go to cancer research and to assist financially-strapped families. We reassured her that she only had to complete a survivors' victory lap at the beginning of the event, and that the youth and volunteers would continue for us through the night. I wasn't surprised when she accepted the offer, especially when I told her that I would bring the frogs.

Relay For Life

The following observation by a former participant compares the one night of a relay walker and the long night of a cancer patient. This unknown author draws a parallel on a small scale between the relay volunteer's exertion and exhaustion in the seemingly endless darkness and the hope ignited by the coming dawn and, corresponding on a much larger scale, the trial that the cancer sufferer endures.

"RELAY FOR LIFE starts at dusk and ends at the next day's morning. The light and darkness of the day and night parallel the physical effects, emotion and mental state of a cancer patient while undergoing treatment.

The relay begins when the sun is setting. This symbolizes the time that the person has been diagnosed as having cancer. The day is getting darker and this represents the cancer patient's state of mind as they feel that their life is coming to an end.

As the evening goes on, it gets colder and darker, just as the emotions of the cancer patient does. Around 1:00 a.m. to 2:00 a.m. represents the time when the cancer patient starts treatment. They become exhausted, some sick, not wanting to go on, possibly wanting to give up. As a participant, we have been walking and feel much the same way. We are tired, want to sleep, maybe even want to go home, but we cannot stop or give up. Around 4:00 a.m. to 5:00 a.m. symbolizes the coming of the end of treatment for the cancer patient. Once again, they are tired, but they know they will make it.

The sun rising represents the end of treatment for the cancer patient. They see the light at the end of the tunnel and know that life will go on. The morning light brings on a new day, full of life and excitement for new beginnings for the cancer patient. As a participant, we will feel the brightness of the morning and know that the end of the RELAY is close at hand.

When we leave the RELAY, we think of the cancer patient leaving their last treatment. Just as we are exhausted and weak, so is that person after treatment."

Susie arrived at the church shortly after Karen and I. While standing outside the sanctuary, we were able to observe almost two hundred high school students preparing for the Relay. They were arriving with every battery-operated entertainment device known to man. Some had pillows while others were sporting blankets and air mattresses. Some even had sleeping bags just in case they were sleepwalking. A live band was setting up on the stage while a DJ was playing CD's, and others were setting up tables with snacks and refreshments. Arrangements were complete.

Just prior to the entrance of the survivors, an announcement was made by one of the student Relay coordinators. "No one will be allowed outside the building between the hours of 10 p.m. and 5 a.m. There will be no consumption of alcohol, smoking or use of profanity. Let's all pull together in support of our friends and loved ones battling cancer."

A signal was given. Debbie Boone's "You Light up My Life" began playing as the survivors entered, carrying a Relay for Life banner and stuffed amphibians, i.e., frogs. I had a hand puppet frog which I caused to wave and make faces as we marched around the circle, lined by young men and women cheering us on, while Gloria Gaynor belted out "I Will Survive." After we passed, the students filled in behind us at the start of what would be a long night.

After our victory lap, we gathered in the front of the church for a group picture that would be presented to the youths in honor of their support. The music grew louder and the kids began skipping, hopping and dancing as they completed their first lap. I said to myself, "I wish I had that kind of energy." Then I thought about it…I don't remember when I had that kind of energy. Life is not wasted on the young. As a survivor, I know that every day is a gift from God and I will live it to its fullest in honor of Him.

***

Susie approached me and said she really appreciated Pastor Karol's sermon and was surprised that one of our pastors was female. Susie went on to remind me that next Sunday was Mother's Day and wanted to know if it would be alright if she brought her daughter and her daughter's boyfriend's mother to church next Sunday. "Of course!" I responded. "The more the merrier."

We are all trying to know, love and serve God and it shouldn't be done alone, for without spiritual guidance, one can rationalize just about anything to justify their actions. We gather in the body as one to worship the Son of God, The Lamb of God, The Light of the World, The Resurrection and the Life, The Bright and Morning Star, Messiah, Holy Spirit, our God Almighty. Before you can share your faith with your fellow man, you must have faith in yourself. I pray that all the children of God will take a knee, not only on Mother's Day, but every day in honor of our Heavenly Father.

***

Susie called me in tears worried about her pending PET scan because she had just seen her doctor and he said, "If it comes back positive, you're toast." She asked, "Why would he say that? I'm hurt because he scared the hell out of me and I've tried to be so positive." I assured her that doctors are human and he might have lost a patient this past week. Perhaps he had lashed out at her because he was helpless and hurting. I told her that I would pray that the PET scan will show negative for cancer and that I would pray for her doctor, who just happens to be my doctor too. I told Susie that after I lost fifty pounds, even with a feeding tube, our doctor had told me, "Sometimes old people just quit eating and die." She chuckled at that remark, and I knew she would be alright.

Several weeks later, the same doctor read the results of her PET scan to her and said, "YOU KICKED CANCER'S ASS!!!" Amen to that. I know Susie will get her saliva glands back and not lose her teeth because I believe in the power of prayer, and my faith in the Lord is a lot bigger than a mustard seed.

FAITH...A LONG ROAD TO A SIMPLE THOUGHT

Faith is believing what you can't see. It comes in all shapes and sizes and can present itself in many forms and varies in strength and weaknesses. A small amount of faith can go a long way, as in Matthew 17:20. *"...if you have faith the size of a mustard seed, you will say to this mountain, 'Move from here to there,' and it will move...*" My wife, Karen, describes her faith as a deep, slow-flowing stream that sometimes disappears below the surface only to re-emerge later and provides a constant source of spiritual power. This cool, pure stream may only quench a few souls' thirst at a time, but the healing powers are phenomenal.

My faith, on the other hand, for most of my life was a dry riverbed. Oh yeah, there may have been some water in it on Sunday mornings and religious holidays, but for the most part, it was dry. How did my faith turn from a dry riverbed to a raging torrent of widespread enthusiasm and passion for the Holy Spirit? The monsoon began when I was diagnosed with cancer.

I was playing in this gigantic sandbox we call life. My faith had as little substance as the sandcastles I built for my family. Wind, rain, rocks and stones from others playing in the sandbox would take their toll on the façade of all that I built. It wasn't until this huge brick called cancer struck my castle that I realized everything I had built for me was made of sand. I climbed out of the sandbox of life carrying that cancerous brick like the proverbial albatross around my neck. I gathered the other stones of experience and went in search of a rock on which to rebuild what was left of my life. I rediscovered the solid rock...Jesus Christ... through prayer and the power of the Holy Spirit. I now realize that I have spent most of my life building my own kingdom and neglected to help God with His. I found a new life in Christ 'Outside the Box' where I could join other Christians showing loving concern through their faithful practice.

One characteristic of faith is that it's contagious and if you're a carrier, it can be passed on to others. Another attribute is that it's magnetic and your faith will draw others of faith to you.

When Karen and I arrived in Wichita, Kansas to work a wind and hail storm that struck the city, we checked in to the historic

Broadview Hotel on the banks of the Arkansas River for an extended stay. Most towns we arrive in don't look their best after an 'act of God'...I prefer natural disaster. The hotel was undergoing its third renovation since it was built in 1922 and we were placed in a room that had yet to be refurbished. The room was clean but the décor was out of the seventies.

One evening when I flushed the toilet, the handle lever broke, dropping the flusher chain to the bottom of the tank. I rolled up my sleeve to check the depth/temperature of the water and pull up on the chain to flush. "Not bad for an eighty-five-year-old building," I thought as I picked up the phone to dial the front desk.

It was almost 9:00 p.m. when there was a tap at the door. Hoping it was the hotel maintenance person, I extricated myself from the soft depths of a sofa that was almost as old as I was and proceeded towards the door. When I opened it, there stood this distinguished-looking, silver-haired gentleman in his sixties, dressed in a white dinner jacket. My first thought was that he might be the emcee from the ballroom downstairs and he inadvertently knocked on the wrong door by mistake. Disappointed he wasn't the hotel maintenance, I inquired, "May I help you?"

The man responded, "I'm with maintenance. You reported a problem with your toilet?" Yes, but in my mind, maintenance guys wore coveralls, either jeans or a work outfit of some kind with their name above the pocket, not a dinner jacket.

The man introduced himself, "I'm Mike. They call me the Preacher of Broadway." Broadway runs north and south through Wichita with the midtown part attracting most of the drug dealers, degenerates, prostitutes and the down-trodden. Mike told us, "I take the gospel to the street on my bicycle, giving the good news to any who will listen. I'm on call for the hotel tonight.

I happened to be at a revival meeting when the maintenance request came in, so I'm a little overdressed for the occasion." He smiled broadly and dashed off to the bathroom.

After a quick inspection, he said, "I'll be right back with the part." When he left, I looked at Karen and said something to the effect that I would have gladly put up with a wet arm rather than drag this man from his service. Mike returned in a few minutes and the repairs were quickly completed.

For some reason, I was compelled to tell Pastor Mike of my spiritual awakening after I was diagnosed with cancer. This impassioned preacher reached out to Karen and me like a mother hen gathering her chicks beneath her wings to shelter them from all peril. Wrapping his arms around our shoulders, he drew us into a circle in the middle of the living room. As we bowed our heads, Preacher Mike began to pray the most powerful prayer I have ever heard. My heart pounded as the benediction began and the Holy Spirit filled the room and descended on this embodied circle. It was as if an elaborate exorcism were pronounced over me to drive away cancer and keep it from ever returning. His prayers intensified in exultation of God's love, power, grace and mercy. To this day, neither Karen nor I can remember a single phrase or sentence of that prayer, but the overwhelming feeling of spirituality still lingers.

After a moment of silence, we broke the circle and stood there simultaneously exhausted and intoxicated with joy and fulfillment. As he prepared to depart, Mike invited us to join him the following Sunday and meet a local pastor called the Chicken Lady. Who would have imagined that such a dirty job as fixing a toilet could be so heavenly? As Karen and I stood there with a blank expression on our faces while looking at one another, a *simple thought* came to mind, "What just happened?"

DIVINE APPOINTMENTS

Late Sunday morning, Karen and I headed to a rendezvous with the renowned Chicken Lady at the old community center on South Broadway. This glory roader, known on the streets as "The Chicken Lady," is an ordained minister. Each Sunday she rents the old community center located in the heart of the down-and-out. Most street people know that every Sunday they can have a hot chicken dinner with dignity and pick up a little "Old Time Religion" to boot…can I get an AMEN? Her mission is to bring a meal and the word of God to the poor and homeless in the face of hopelessness.

When he gave us directions to the gathering place, Preacher Mike had cautioned us, "Keep your car doors locked until you arrive at the center and make sure all of your valuables are in the trunk, out of sight. The only things I bring with me when I'm preaching on Broadway are my Bible and my bike…I'm on my third bike."

As we pulled into the parking lot, the bedraggled and disheveled children of God were beginning to gather outside the doors. While passing through this motley group of the downtrodden and impoverished, a feeling of fear and despair came over me. I wanted to turn my eyes away from that gathering of the downtrodden, but who am I - for they are the ones to be honored today? *"For I was hungry, and you gave Me something to eat; I was thirsty, and you gave Me something to drink; I was a stranger, and you invited Me in." Matthew 25:35* We would be gathered together as one body to share life, the Lord's Supper and breaking of bread, for God is the sovereign Father of us all. Running the gauntlet of men wreathed in cigarette smoke, I held my breath until we were safely inside.

Apparently we had arrived before Preacher Mike, but the Chicken Lady wasn't hard to find. Already at work orchestrating like a drill sergeant, she was instructing volunteers as to their duties, and giving training lessons to the newbies that would be working the serving line. She was a medium-height, stocky African-American with sturdy legs and a face as radiant as an angel's. The pastor was wearing a black dress and jacket with modest jewelry and a name tag between her lapel and right breast pocket. As Karen and I approached this woman of God, her attention turned from her volunteers. Casting a brilliant smile in our direction, she introduced herself as Pastor Dee while clasping each of our hands in turn. (At least she didn't refer to herself as 'Chicken Lady.') While looking upon the face of this ecclesiastic servant of God, I felt that something awe-inspiring was about to take place. As Mother Teresa often told people who would like to serve the poor, "What I can do, you cannot. What you can do, I cannot. But together we can do something beautiful for God." (Mother Teresa's message to the Fourth Women's Conference.)

This scene brought vividly to mind something my sister had given me to read when I was so very ill. My brother, Jeff, succumbed to cancer on Christmas morning several years ago, after a short but rather intense battle. Just prior to his death, he wrote an essay on mankind. This was what my sister brought to me:

Mankind

> We are borne in darkness and confusion, into this world we are brought hungry and naked. Our first needs are those of the beast — hunger, warmth.

> From that time on we must search for our place in the, "march of mankind."

> Some, it seems, early in life, are not strong enough to join the "march." Our Father calls their souls back.

For those who survive, the "march" has begun and with it their search for fulfillment of their lives. As man matures he slowly, dimly realizes the role he must fulfill in life. He sees that he and mankind are one; in that they all spring from the same seed.

It matters not that a man be black, white, red, yellow, nor that he be a teacher, blacksmith, drunkard or soldier.

Within each man exists a silent knowledge of himself and all men.

We should spend an hour each day meditating upon this gift, and let a quarter of that hour be in prayer for the revealing light of knowledge to pierce the smothering veil of ignorance.

One hour in fruitful thought is better than a year of striving for worldly gains.

I say to you there is a frightening degree of ignorance in this world.

If you say to a man:

Why do you let great books lay unread? Why do you walk down the street with your eyes veiled to nature's beauty? Why do you deafen your ears to the laughter of children? Why do you deaden your soul to the pleas of the downtrodden?

All too often comes the answer:

"I haven't the time."

Jesus of Nazareth had the time, Confucius had the time. Their names are spoken with reverence throughout the world. Yet we, with our pitiful, tiny lives, have not the time.

Never do you see the trees or flowers unless nature takes up her breath and bludgeons you with the aroma of the flowers.

With the coming of your children you swell with pride, but all too soon they lose their newness.

They are not toys!

One day they shall inherit that which you today build.

The man who lost his legs, the animal, the alcoholic; it seems that they are not of the human family.

How do you find it so easy to pass them on the street without a deep love for them?

Remember this:

Even as the Holy and Righteous cannot rise above the highest which is in you,

So, the wicked and the weak cannot fall lower than the lowest which is in you, also.

I leave you with this thought.....

Never can you lose your dignity as a man, nor can you lose your love of life, unless you, yourself murder it.

Jeff Bradford

For the first time I was on the inside of humanity looking out rather than looking down from my lofty perch of self-righteousness. I know that I'm guilty of thumbing my condescending nose at the "dregs of humanity." Cancer taught me that sometimes one must sink deep into a state of hopelessness and apathy before the seed of hope can grow. Now I understand why learning from life's experiences is called "The School of Hard Knocks." Life hit me so hard it knocked the stuffing out of me. It's not until you've been there and done that and experienced disheartenment before you can honestly say, "I know how you feel," but you still won't know. Once this void was created in me, it made a lot of room for humble pie and the words of God. As I began to study the Bible, I learned to trust in the words…not just read the words on the page…but rather *lift* them from the page and teach them to my brothers and sisters. The Lord has told me, "I gave you two ears and one mouth," to remind me that I should talk less and listen more. But sometimes I get so much enthusiasm while spreading the gospel, he has to remind me to listen…children.

It turned out that Pastor Dee was short-handed on the serving line, so she asked Karen and me if we could assist. That humble pie was sure starting to taste good as I lapped up the opportunity to serve those I had just judged. After a few last minutes of instructions, the doors were opened and our guests began arriving. As they were filing in, I noticed that the large body of pressing humanity that had gathered outside began to have faces, and soon, names. One by one they stood before me with arms outstretched, each with their own smiles and words of gratitude and blessings. I never realized my heart would be so humbled in their presence. Not one that passed before me failed to thank me, bless me and thank God. Those who couldn't or wouldn't speak did so with their smiles and the bowing of their heads in gratitude. If there is no hope here, then where is there hope? As Pastor Dee said the blessing, I said a blessing of my own while listening. *"The Lord bless you and keep you! The Lord make his face to shine upon you and be gracious unto you! The Lord lift up his countenance upon you and give you peace!" Numbers 6:24-26*

Pastor Dee held no one bondservant to her preaching by withholding the feast until after the Word. Rather she provided "angel food" after the meal to those wanting the dessert of Christ Jesus to quench iniquitous deeds of the past. More than two hundred men, women and children were served (some twice) prior to today's message which was about "faith."

Over half of the collective body remained for the words of encouragement and hope that Pastor Dee was about to invoke. We were each given a small zip lock bag that appeared empty, except that further study revealed a tiny mustard seed. Most had no idea what this small speck was in the bag as they held it up to the light, cocking a head to one side in further study with facial expressions of wonderment. Something as small and of as little value as this tiny seed has the possibility of catching many fish from this small pond of humanity. Thanks, Pastor Dee, for the abundance of angel food to nurture our faith and nourish our soul.

RIDING FOR THE SON

While sitting in the car waiting to board the Washington ferry from Anacortes to Sidney on Vancouver Island, I thought that we could finally relax and enjoy a desperately needed two-week vacation. Our plan was to see the Butchart Gardens in Victoria, British Columbia then go sailing in the San Juan Islands for a week with friends on their fifty-two foot Catalina. Maybe we'd do a little salmon fishing, some crabbing for Dungeness. But best of all, there would be no phones, no TV … just plain relaxing.

The past two years had been a nightmarish blur of eighty-plus-hour-work weeks away from home, a battle almost lost to cancer and a flurry of medical appointments with matching bills. Now, in a dreamy stupor, I watched the ferry named Tillikum (from Chinook for "friends/relatives") pull into the landing with horns blasting her arrival. This wasn't our maiden voyage aboard the Washington State ferry system, but every ferry trip awakens the excited little boy in me. I was looking forward to running from stem to stern. While Karen relaxed on the observation deck, I'd hang out in the stern.

I followed the directions of the deck attendants onto the massive auto deck, crowding in with other vehicles in an efficient maneuver that seems to take just moments. Setting the emergency brake, I could already feel the gentle rolling motion of the ferry as the massive diesels roared and vibrated under my feet. Once we were out of the car, it was a tight squeeze maneuvering around the parked cars in the dimly lit car deck to reach the stairs. But there is a front row seat to the world waiting up top. I did the man thing and escorted Karen upstairs to the glass-enclosed observation room about half the length and width of a football field. Karen settled into a booth next to a wall-sized window as I proceeded towards the mess hall…I mean the culinary department…to scrounge up something to eat during the short trip.

After a quick bite, I proceeded towards the bow, exchanging a friendly wave to the helmswoman in the pilot house. Wait a minute! A woman driving a 310'x73' ship with 2,500 horse-power? You go, girl! If you're pushing 2070 tons of iron, most will get out of your way.

It was early September and there was a nip of fall in the moist air as we crossed the Strait of Juan de Fuca. Standing under the pilot house on the lee side, I could look down at the auto deck and see the waves splashing at the bow created by our forward motion. While I was gazing across the straits towards Sidney, I noticed a couple of motorcycle dudes hanging around a Harley below on the auto deck. They were sporting the typical leather jackets, denim and boots like Marlon Brando in The Wild Ones. There was something intriguingly different about the patches known as "colors" on the back of their jackets. The words Christian Motorcyclist Association formed a triangle around a black Bible with a white cross on the cover and clasped hands in prayer at the bottom of the cross. There were two ribbon banners in an arc. The one across the top of the triangle had the words "Riding — For" and the bottom rocker said "The Son." The "colors" were blue, yellow and black lettering and red trim. They wore no oth-er insignia of the sort one would expect from Hell's Angels gang members, or were these Heaven's Angels? "Who are these guys?" I wondered as I returned to Karen on the observation deck.

A short time later Karen jabbed me with her elbow and nodded to a group of passengers headed toward the bow. "That's pretty cool," she said. It was the same group of motorcyclists I had spotted on the parking deck. We speculated about the meaning of the emblems on the jackets but couldn't muster the courage or the energy to leave the mesmerizing comfort of our seat by the window. After the ferry docked we watched them ride off in the flock of motorcycles that were allowed to disembark before the other vehicles.

After the Tillikum had disgorged her payload on Vancouver Island, we went in search of the butterfly house and gardens. The butterfly house was like a tropical forest with streams, waterfalls and small ponds. There were over a hundred species and a thousand butterflies. The adults, like the children, were mesmerized by the rainbow colors of fluttering wings. I watched a little girl hold her breath as one landed on her outstretched finger while another landed on my head. We had lots of fun but it was time to grab lunch and head for the Butchart Gardens. We were burning daylight.

It was early afternoon when we arrived at the gardens and the weather was picture perfect. A fairly large crowd had come to the gardens to drink in the last of the summer colors before the trees dressed themselves for autumn. After we paid the ten dollars for parking, we were directed to the proverbial back forty where we would get in a respectable walk on our way to the main gates. We were some distance from where we parked the car when Karen asked the dreaded question, "Did you bring the camera?"

No need for a response from me. "I'll go get it. Besides I don't think I'll need my sweater. You wait here," Karen said as she headed back to the car for the camera while I admired a cedar hedge that had to be over twenty feet high. Then, there they were, those same motorcycle dudes I saw on the ferry early this morning. They had just paid their parking fee and found a parking spot close to the entrance. I was drawn to them like a lodestone for I had to find the answer to this burning desire in my mind to know, "Who are these guys?"

They were in the process of removing their helmets when I approached them. After a short introduction, they let me know that they were God's messengers not hell raisers. One of them commented, "These are our 'church clothes,'" as he gestured to his riding apparel. "We follow strict rules. No drinking. No smoking. No drugs. No profanity."

Led by the Holy Spirit, these road warriors for Christ spread the gospel with a bike, a Bible and a prayerful blessing. While motorcycle gangs have territories, "Riding for the Son" covers all of God's turf. The "Wheels of Faith" Christian ministry, like the spokes of a wheel, goes out in all directions. Most ride Harleys but others have Hondas, Suzukis, Yamahas and Kawasakis as they reach out to all, whether they know or don't know Jesus.

These road riders seek the lost or wayward children. Their motorcycles provide a stealth entrance into the subculture, allowing them to approach the unapproachable, breaking down the barriers that have been built against faith and religion. The Christian Motorcyclist Association (CMA) is not a substitute for church. It's more like an outreach program to draw Christians to know, love and serve Christ in a church or a place of worship.

The CMA are "Holy Rollers," not to be confused with "God's Squad (UK)" or "Cycle Disciples." They are neither a club nor a gang but rather a ministry for Christ. Jesus was somewhat of a rebel and nonconformist. He drank and hung out with society's outcasts, tax collectors and prostitutes. Would he ride a Harley? These riders for Christ come from all walks of life for they are teachers, doctors, lawyers and grandparents. The CMA members are involved in many different ministries from helping the homeless, to prison visits, and youth work.

It takes a special person to reach out to non-believers and former believers who have, for whatever reason, gone underground. There is a lot of pain and suffering in the dregs of society. CMA members are rather like the Johnny Appleseed of Christianity. They scatter the seeds of faith as they travel among the hardened and skeptical, watering them with their prayers. Then they leave the rest to God. Some of the seeds will sprout. Some of the seeds will wither. But without the seed, there is no hope for a harvest. *"And He spoke many things to them in parables, saying, 'Behold, the sower went out to sow; and as he sowed, some seeds fell beside the road, and the birds came and ate them up. Others fell on the rocky places, where they did not have much soil; and immediately they sprang up, because they had no depth of soil. But when the sun had risen, they were scorched; and because they had no root, they withered away. Others fell among the thorns, and the thorns came up and choked them out. And others fell on the good soil and yielded a crop, some a hundredfold, some sixty, and some thirty.' "* *Matthew 13:3-8*

In a circle of leather jackets, boots and one pair of sneakers, we wrapped our arms around one another, bowed our heads and prayed. We became that conduit the Holy Spirit uses to reach out to his children. These were heaven's angels. When we were done praying, they donned their helmets, mounted their bikes and left the park. I stood there puzzled. They had just arrived, so why were they leaving? It was as if their only purpose for entering the gardens was to rendezvous and pray with me. Perhaps the real reason was that God wanted me to tell their story. *"For Christ did not send me to baptize, but to preach the gospel, not in cleverness of speech, so that the cross of Christ would not be made void. For the word of the cross is foolishness to those who are perishing, but to us who are being saved it is the power of God."* *1 Corinthians 1:17-18*

Karen arrived as they were riding off, but she had witnessed the prayer circle from a distance. I asked her if she was surprised to find me praying with motorcycle dudes, and she responded, "Nothing you do surprises me anymore."

Moriarty

Professor James Moriarty, archenemy of Sherlock Holmes, is the villain in a classic mystery but the story I'm about to tell is better than a mystery; it's a true story. After three months working in Kansas City, twelve-hour shifts six days a week, it's time to head west, young man, back to Arizona. With the car packed, to my chagrin, I still felt as if I were forgetting something like the kitchen sink. My sister was born in Kansas, and Karen and I liked Wichita. But after working there for three months, the best-looking thing about Kansas was Wichita in my rear view mirror. An early start and high hopes of making the seven hundred plus miles to Albuquerque seemed tough but doable.

It was early October and the days were growing shorter in preparation for those long winter nights. Surrounded by darkness and lacking the eagle eye of my youth, I asked Karen to search the map for a place to stop since we were still more than a hundred miles from Albuquerque. We were tired and had just outrun a big, bad thunderstorm in the Texas panhandle. Eureka! Moriarty another fifty clicks down the road. Mortuary...? I told Karen that I was looking for a respite not a permanent resting place.

When we rolled in to Moriarty, the place was packed and all four of the major hotels were booked. It seems that Moriarty's biggest event of the year was taking place: the crowning of the Pinto Bean Queen...really. Physically unable to proceed further and not wanting to sleep in the car, we asked each hotel if they knew of any available accommodations. One young receptionist pierced with two rings through her lower lip (I think that's called a snake bite) and covered in tattoos, shrugged her shoulders and shook her head no. As we were leaving the hotel, I wondered why they would hire a mute as a receptionist.

Moriarty is a small town with a population around eighteen hundred and, aside from the Pinto Bean Festival, I don't think much else happens other than the coming and going of weary travelers from the interstate. In search of any port in the storm, we drove away from the freeway exit through town.

Through the dark and gloom of night, right out of a sixties' Hitchcock flick, a dimly lit VACANCY sign appeared. Desperate, we pulled in and made our way to the office, which was a closed-in porch with a steel barred window next to a buzzer and sign that dared me to "press for assistance." Reluctantly I pushed the button to summon the caretaker. The buzzing of the red neon vacancy sign drew my attention to the pathetic old marquee in front. I somehow expected it to say "George Washington Slept Here," rather than "rooms for let by week." I was somewhat startled when a man inquired in a deep voice, "May I help you?"

"Yes, ah, ah… I was wondering if you still had a vacancy and if so, may I check out the room first?" Handing me the key, he pointed to his left. Rest assured, I knew I would not get lost in an L-shaped, one-story, fifteen-room motel.

The decor was fit for a novice's cell in a contemplative order. You could say spartan: bed, lamp, end-table, desk/dresser. No, the TV was not black and white with rabbit ears, but I don't think it was worth stealing either. Flopping on the bed, we found it to be soft but at least it wasn't a "hotdog bun"…you know, the bed that flips up on both sides as you slowly sink to the floor in the middle. All in all, the room was clean, and after all, we weren't going to buy the place. Not wanting to leave our things in the room, Karen paid cash for the night, and we went out to rustle up something to eat. When we returned to the motel, Karen retrieved her overnight bag. Not wanting to unload the large suitcase from the trunk, I placed my nose under my armpit, and with a snort, I proclaimed I was good for another four hundred miles in the morning. The only problem was my Bible was in that suitcase. No problem, I knew the Gideons would not let me down.

There it was, just as I knew it would be, tucked in the corner of the nightstand. But there was something different about this particular Gideon's Bible…it was worn. While retrieving the Bible from the nightstand, I figured that either this Bible had been here since the motel was built or some "harp polisher" got a hold of it. Perhaps many a weary traveler had seized it to find refuge from the "sin hound," for the Word and the Cross can repair the irreparable. Nevertheless, this Bible definitely had some heavy mileage on it and I was about to find out why.

Normally when I open my Bible, I proceed to my bookmark and continue where I had left off the previous day, unless I was looking something up. For some reason, I opened this Bible to the very first page. I did not realize that I was about to embark on an abbreviated journey through redemption to salvation. An unknown cleric had marked this Bible to make it a treasure map rather than a labyrinthine enigma.

The carefully orchestrated tour of the Bible began at "the beginning," Genesis 1:1, and continued through John, Revelation and ended with a simple prayer written in the margin in Romans 10. *"…but just as we have been approved by God to be entrusted with the gospel, so we speak, not as pleasing men, but God who examines our hearts." 1 Thessalonians 2:4*

We wanted to preserve that message, so Karen photographed the pertinent pages. The Bible itself remained in the nightstand next to the bed, waiting for any and all that seek Him. To me, finding that Bible will always be the biggest event to occur in the blessed town of Moriarty.

DIVINE APPOINTMENTS

The blank page preceding the Book of Genesis contained a handwritten outline which included specific pages to be read:

> #1: God
> "The Beginning"
> Genesis (Book # 1)
>   Chapter 1
>   Verse 1
> Go to John
>   John 1:1
> Go to Revelation 1:8
>   I am …The Beginning
> Jesus Christ, The Beginning of all things.
> He is the pattern of all creation showing The
> Perfect Salvation
>   Go to John 3:16
> Go to Romans 3:23

On the first page next to the title, Genesis, was a hand-written addition "= Beginning of Life," the writer annotated verses 1-5 emphasizing that "in the beginning" God was the Creator. The first thing God speaks into existence is Light and the notation compares Light to understanding. God then divides the light from the darkness. The *evening* and the *morning* are the first day, which are compared to "death/burial" and "resurrection."

Next, we were sent to the Gospel of John, which our guide had subtitled "God is Gracious." The writer emphasized the parallels between Genesis and The Gospel of John. John, like Genesis, begins with the words, "In the beginning." In annotations from verse 1 through verse 17, the writer shows us that as God made the world, Jesus, The Word, was with God "in the beginning" and that Jesus is God and through Him all things were made. In the margin of the text we were instructed that "Word" can also mean "Promise;" when someone gives their word, they make a promise. John goes on to say that The Word was life and light – remember the life and light connections in Genesis. Here we have the wonderful news that Jesus gave the right/power "*to become children of God, to those who believe in His name.*" *John 1:12* John then addresses God's grace and how we receive that grace.

> 14 And *the Word became flesh and dwelt among us, and we beheld His glory, the glory as of the only begotten of the Father, full of grace and truth*.

> …

> 16 *And of His fullness we have all received, and grace for grace*.

> 17 For the law was given through Moses, but *grace and truth came through Jesus Christ.*

In Revelation, our guide took us to the part of the first chapter where Jesus Christ is called "the faithful witness, the firstborn from the dead." We are told that He "loved us and washed us from our sins in His own blood."

Then we returned to the Gospel of John, chapter 3 where we read the story of Nicodemus, to whom Jesus explained the concept of being born again to be able to see the kingdom of God. During the instruction of Nicodemus we find the wonderful verse 16:

"*For God so loved the world, that He gave His only begotten Son, that whoever believes in Him shall not perish, but have eternal life.*" *John 3:16*

The final book of instruction was Romans, beginning with chapter 3 verse 23. We were reminded that none of us can live up to the letter of the law and all have sinned, but that we can be justified by grace through Jesus Christ. In chapter 5 we were told that God showed his love for us in that "*while we were still sinners Christ died for us.*" Chapter 6 verse 23 tells us that our own efforts can only earn us death (the wages of sin) but eternal life is a *gift* from God through His Son Jesus Christ. Chapter 10 was where our guide ended the instruction with these words, hand-written in the margins:

"Salvation comes freely by simply believing and receiving God's free gift. A simple prayer = Lord Jesus, please forgive me and come into my life and save me. Thank you."

PART 3

COMPUSION TO WRITE

Compulsion to Write

In May of 2007, Karen was assigned to work a hail event in Columbus, Ohio. I joined her there; but since this operation had been in place for many months, all the jobs were filled. There was no position for me in the office.

I enjoy walking and there were some nice pathways around the area we were staying. Ponds, lush with cattails, reeds, and lotus, populated with ducks and geese and, yes, frogs, were a pleasant diversion for me. But at this time I began to feel an intense urging to write down everything that had happened to me.

This intense urging became a mandate, an obsession. I knew I had to write it. As I said in the preface, I didn't want to. But we had our laptop computer with us and I had plenty of time on my hands. That's when I began to record everything that has preceded this part of the book.

I prayed diligently over each part I needed to write. I searched my heart and my mind. I checked facts with Karen. Of course, many of these stories carried such deep meaning for me that I had shared them with many individuals. Much repetition had made them as an oral history for me, clear in content, detail and phrasing. So writing became my occupation and walking my diversion until Karen's assignment ended.

TITUS

After working in Columbus for three months, Karen was released and we prepared to fly back to Flagstaff. With an early flight and the three-hour time difference traveling east to west, it was going to be a long day. Karen and I dropped the rental car off, checked our luggage, made it through security, and arrived at the gate with surprising ease. We looked around the crowded waiting room for a couple of seats together, preferably away from foot traffic. Almost simultaneously we spotted what appeared to be the only two seats together, with an end table separating them from a nice-looking man who appeared to be of Filipino or Hawaiian descent.

As we made our way to the open seats, I couldn't help but stare at the young man because he possessed an engrossed look of rapt delight. His smile was intense and he seemed suffused with an aura of majestic presence. We both were intuitively drawn in by this man with a grin worthy of the Cheshire Cat in <u>Alice in Wonderland</u>. Without introduction the man turned towards us and with pressured speech blurted out, "God spoke to me this morning." Still smiling, he admitted that previously, when people told him they had been visited by the Holy Spirit or had heard the word of God, he would tell them that the only way God speaks to us is through His Word in the Holy Bible. But now he proclaimed, "I know that I heard the Lord God at four forty-five this morning."

I had no trouble believing this child of God, for I too have been visited by the Holy Spirit and have heard the word of God. I, too, was excited and humbled after that divine visit, but I don't know if I would have blurted it out to strangers in an airport… who knows, maybe I would. This man's exuberance was equal to or even surpassed by his radiance that enveloped him with the atmosphere of the Holy Spirit. After a short introduction, he said his name was Titus, like in the Bible, and he was traveling to Arizona to visit a sister whom he hadn't seen in over twenty years. Titus told us he lived in Columbus but was originally from the Philippines where another sister was still residing. I glanced over at Karen and I could see that she was just as intrigued with this man as I.

Titus began his captivating story about his older sister, Maria, in the Philippines and her dear friend and next-door neighbor, Bonita, who suffered a heart attack a few weeks earlier. Among other challenges in her life, Bonita had a child as a result of an affair with a married man. With Maria's help, she had found the Lord and was trying to change her life. Both Maria and Titus were praying fervently for Bonita's healing, as well as the Lord's salvation and forgiveness for her.

Titus had already made plans to visit his sister in Arizona when Maria called him with the bad news that Bonita was in the hospital and her recovery looked bleak. He had thought of changing his plans but decided against it because of a deep desire to be with the sister whom he hadn't seen in over twenty years.

However, Titus told us that through prayer he found himself vehemently bargaining with the Lord for Bonita's recovery since he believed she needed more time to accomplish the cleansing of her soul. I think that most of us are guilty of allowing Satan to con us into an attempt to play 'tit for tat' with the Lord. "God, if you will only give me this job or promotion, I promise to attend church every Sunday or fast or be a nicer person." This isn't to say that you can't pray passionately for the Lord's help for guidance and understanding. But He really doesn't need anything from us and He already knows what we truly need from Him.

The previous evening while packing for his trip, Titus received a call from Maria. Bonita had died. Titus told us that he worked at an auto parts warehouse and this was his first vacation in a while. Now he was torn between a desire to comfort the one sister in the loss of her best friend and a promise he made to another sister he vaguely remembered. "All I could do," he said, "was to go to the Lord in prayer."

Titus related that he had gone to bed praying and continued to pray for Bonita whenever he woke during a restless night. While he was in intense spiritual introspection and prayer, Titus asked the Holy Spirit why Bonita wasn't given more time to cleanse the sins from her soul. He had been praying fervently for her recovery and salvation and now it seemed her opportunity was lost. That was when the Holy Spirit spoke to Titus and said, *"Bonita was with the father for eighteen hours when I held my arm out to her and said, 'Reach up and touch my arm and you can return to the world you know.' But she would not."*

Once more Titus asked the Holy Spirit why Bonita wasn't given more time to repent for her sins. Again the Holy Spirit spoke, *"With the Father, she was without sin. Again I held out my arm to her to take her back to the world and she refused. She was afraid she would sin again."*

Titus said that he was wide awake by this time. He glanced at the clock and saw it was 4.45 a.m. He was sad for Maria because he knew she would miss her friend. But now he was at peace knowing that Bonita was in the arms of God.

Karen left her seat to check out one of the gift shops in the airport while I told Titus how the Holy Spirit snatched me from death's door. I told him a few frog stories and what F.R.O.G. stood for and how cancer saved my soul. We bowed our heads and took turns glorifying God through prayer in a confession of faith.

When Karen returned she whispered to me that there was a stuffed frog in the gift shop. I excused myself telling them I was in need of a pit stop before I boarded the plane. While true, this also freed me for a quick trip to the gift shop to capture a frog for my brother in Christ. I returned and presented the stuffed frog to Titus. He was almost in tears as he returned that Cheshire grin.

With an affectionate embrace, we bid farewell as we prepared to board the plane. While in line, I glanced over my shoulder; I could see Titus off to the side looking down at his frog, smiling and grasping it with both hands.

KISMET

I think we're all familiar with serendipity but what about foreordained fate? Will a predestined messenger arrive at his or her destiny by fate or godsend? Both ways, an esoteric message belongs to the "secret things" of God, and He alone controls and directs these events by his messengers. God uses all of his children as a conduit to deliver His message to us. The most powerful messenger is the Son of God.

In late August of 2007, Karen was between assignments. It was the first day of school for Nizhoni my five-year-old granddaughter and, unfortunately, my son and daughter-in-law failed to update her shot record and she would not be allowed to attend. It turned out she would need five shots to be caught up before they would allow her in the "garden of children" (kindergarten). With classes beginning at nine, my wife and I picked up Nizhoni just before eight in hopes of getting her to the clinic for her shots so she wouldn't miss her first day of school. Nizhoni knew we were taking her to get the dreaded SHOTS! Out of nervousness, she was talking a lot more than usual. Perhaps it was the dream of being a grownup and attending school like her older brother and sister. We didn't realize that something as simple as a few shots was about to become a quest.

We arrived at the Community Health Clinic shortly after eight and got in a long line behind people coughing and sneezing. I must say it didn't look too promising as some of the sick were curled up in their chairs as if they had spent the night there. My immune system has never recovered since the battle with cancer and I was afraid I might catch something if we hung around there any longer. Karen spotted a sign that read, "Shot clinic Tuesday and Thursday." With this being Monday, I was happy to get out of this place. On the way out the door, a young couple who overheard our conversation said we might have some luck with First Care or Concentra. Both facilities wanted us to schedule an appointment with one of their doctors because Nizhoni was a new patient. If she was old enough to join the Army, she would get all her shots for free. Out of time constaints and desperation, Karen called our family doctor. His nurse told us they don't stock children's vaccines since they deal only with adults. She directed us to another possibility at a nearby well clinic.

With a few directions and a couple of wrong turns we managed to find the well clinic, and I must say it looked promising for there was only one person waiting in the dimly lit back corner. It was now after nine and school had just started. I proceeded to the window and explained my granddaughter's plight. I was informed that since she was a new patient, she would first have to make an appointment to see one of their doctors.

Desperate, I began my plea about the importance of the first day of school. I asked if there was any way they could work her in. Hoping I could convince them to see her, I went on to say that next to your wedding day, your first day of school is a "most important day." I noticed four brown American Cancer Society shirts draped across the back of the office chairs. I told them I was a cancer survivor and that next week I would carry my stuffed frog up the mountain in a backpack. I explained the significance of F.R.O.G. – Fully Rely On God, and how through prayer and the power of the Holy Spirit I was able to battle cancer.

My song and dance availed me nothing. But they said that maybe the Children's Health Center at the main hospital would be able to administer her shots. They said good luck and they would see me next week climbing the mountain to conquer cancer. As we were leaving the clinic, I again noticed the man dressed in cowboy attire with an oxygen tube calmly waiting in the corner.

After we had made our way to the Children's Health Center on the second floor, Karen handed the receptionist Nizhoni's shot record as we waited for the verdict. We were asked to be seated and shortly a nurse came out with the good news. Apparently Nizhoni had been seen there before. They would work her in, but it might take some time. I explained the first day of school thing and the nurse just smiled and said she knew for she had children and grandchildren also.

Nizhoni seemed excited with the prospect of finally getting the shots over with and getting to school. An hour passed, which is an eternity if you are a small child waiting for shots, but finally we were called to the back. The nurse said she was able to combine two of the shots so that Nizhoni would get two in her left and two in the right arm. A lot braver than I, she wiggled a little bit and a small tear formed in the corner of her eyes as she said,

"No more shots. I want to go to school!" She shook it off like a trooper. Then with a sip of liquid Tylenol for aches and fever and the gift of a small toy, she was more than ready for school.

Karen and I grabbed her hand and took off with our one thought being to get the child to her first day of school before lunch. As we were crossing the hospital parking lot, a man jumped out of the passenger's side of a pickup and shouted, "Did your granddaughter get her shots?" Surprised and somewhat thrown off guard by this man in cowboy garb, I realized he was the one we had seen in the well clinic an hour and a half ago. With a smile I answered, "Yes and we're off to school."

The man told me his name and said his wife was in the pharmacy picking up morphine for him. He was dying from cancer and had less than a month to live. He said he had heard my story at the clinic and with both arms extended palms up he pleaded, "Teach me to F.R.O.G." I was a new disciple for Christ and I failed this man for I did not reach out and grab his hands in prayer. Instead I gave him my name and number and said I would meet with him for prayer. He never called and I was unable to locate him, so I continue to pray alone for his redemption and my forgiveness.

When your soul is called from you, where will you spend eternity? *"...that if you confess with your mouth Jesus as Lord, and believe in your heart that God raised Him from the dead, you will be saved." Romans 10:9*

I pray to the Lord to forgive my callowness and teach me so that I may teach others as I carry the cross of my own spiritual blindness. If I only would have told this man who reached out to me, "If you accept Christ Jesus as your Lord and Savior, take my hands and pray with me," I would have given him this prayer:

My Lord, God and Father, I trust in the blood of your Son Christ Jesus to cleanse me from sin. I believe Christ died for me and rose from the dead. I repent of my sins and will trust in Jesus to take me to be with you in heaven. I accept you as my Lord and Savior in Jesus' name, amen.

I knew that this man's last days would be hard and long, but he would not have to face them alone. I pray I will meet one day with this soul to praise God for all eternity. Today I find comfort in those heart-wrenching words, "teach me to F.R.O.G." Even though I let my brother down, I prayed then and still do that Jesus walked with him the rest of the way. The Lord knows I'm young in my faith and I pray He has forgiven me.

USHERS

I have served as an usher at our church for over fifteen years. The pay is constant, you won't be fired, and you can't quit. While our family was out of town on vacation, we missed two Sunday services in a row. When we returned I found out the Administrative Council had voted me in as President of the Board of Trustees. I was afraid to miss another Council meeting for fear they would vote me onto the Finance Committee or something.

While visiting with the Choir Director, James Kirk, I jokingly told him that the reason I'm an usher is that if I attempt to sing a hymn, I won't offend anyone because I'm in the back of the church. James apparently didn't get my little pun because he looked at me real seriously and asked me if I could sing tenor. Somewhat embarrassed, I responded, "I don't know… I never tried." With a chuckle, he said, "Try singing *ten-or*-twelve miles from here." At least he didn't ask me if I could sing solo...*so low* that no one can hear me.

I find that ushering is quite rewarding, serving the Lord's children while honoring Him. While greeting your church family with handshakes and hugs, there is great anticipation for the glory of worshiping our Father. As one, we become a bright shining gloriole around the collective body, exulting with triumph over Satan. Deuteronomy 32:30 teaches us, *"How could one chase a thousand, And two put ten thousand to flight, Unless their Rock had sold them, And the LORD had given them up?"* Our Lord will not forsake us, for we are made Holy through Sanctifying Grace and the Sacrament of Holy Communion. One man-child of God, while waiting in line for the Eucharist, whispered in my ear, "Is it free?" Knowing the ultimate price that Jesus paid, I responded, "Of course it's free. It's Angel food."

After the loss of my good friend and fellow usher, Ray Johnston, I was asked if I would usher Ray's celebration of life memorial. With reverence and a heavy heart, I graciously accepted this honor to pay tribute to my brother in Christ. Saddened, I also reflected on my comrade, Bob Allen, with whom I had ushered for over ten years and who had died six months earlier from Alzheimer's. The joy of looking upon another one's face and knowing you will spend eternity together, glorifying God, provides enough consolation as I still grieve their loss.

I had met with Ray just six weeks ago, and we discussed the recent loss of his bride of sixty-one years. Ray told me that he had battled brain cancer and melanoma for the past ten years, and the fight is now over. Ray said he was ready to see the Lord and just a few weeks later, he died of a broken heart. Not even cancer could take him from his bride, but his bride took him from cancer. *"The Spirit and the bride say, 'Come.' And let the one who hears say, 'Come.' And let the one who is thirsty come; let the one who wishes take the water of life without cost." Revelation 2:17*

The families gathered in the narthex where several of Rays landscape oil paintings were on display along with memorable photographs. I remembered seeing his paintings in the living and dining rooms when we had visited Ray and Cathy. The ceremony began as I proceeded down the aisle towards the altar to light the candles. I was suffering great sorrow for the loss of my friend as I approached the altar. But a smile soon came to my face as I began to light the candles. I imagined Ray and Cathy walking down the aisle sixty-one years ago to share their lives in matrimony and faith. I reflected that I had been blessed to walk down the aisle with Ray every week for over two years. After lighting the candles, I turned from the altar and as I faced the congregation, I heard Ray whisper in my ear, "I will meet you in the aisle and walk with you again to the altar of God to worship Him for eternity." I bowed my head as I extinguished the flame from the wand and thanked the Lord for such a dear friend.

ANGELA

The reason we're called patients while waiting in a doctor's office is that's what we must have...patience. Karen and I were patiently waiting at my ophthalmologist's office to check the status of my pigmentary glaucoma and see if something could be done about the cataracts that had formed in both of my eyes. My stuffed fuzzy frog, Rad, had accompanied us as he has during numerous visits to the doctor. We were soon met with a cordial greeting and a familiar hug by a technician named Angela. She was well aware of my past history of glaucoma and the many eye problems as a result of an earlier seizure during my treatments for cancer.

After she had ushered us into the exam room, Angela began screening in preparation for the doctor. We engaged in trivial conversation about each other, our families and of course my frog, Rad. Angela's playful conversation became more deliberate and turned very serious when she told me that her younger sister, Mandy, succumbed to cancer when they were both very young. Apparently they were inseparable companions and the best of friends who did virtually everything together. As cancer began to ravage Mandy's young body, the frightened child went to Angela's room late one night. The disheartened little girl did not want to be alone with a voracious monster so terrorizing, grotesque and horribly wicked as cancer. Secure in Angela's embrace, Mandy was comforted and she slept, believing her big sister could defend her from cancer's onslaught. But cancer soon took its toll on Mandy's frail little body until one night, in the middle of the night, she cried out in anguish and defeat while reaching for Angela's comforting embrace. Smiling through her tears, Angela told me that Mandy left her arms that night for God's.

I was deeply moved and dismayed; my heavy heart was made humble by Angela's immense sweeping pain over her loss. My own troubles turned to vapors as I began to fathom her tremendous love she shared with Mandy. How could I reach out to this woman who would confide and entrust in me the grave pain inflicted by her loss? I feel that she may have been encouraged by my faith as I was by hers. If you notice someone carrying a Bible around with them, one may automatically assume they are spiritual in their beliefs and devotion to the Lord. How about someone carrying an unassuming stuffed frog? Sometimes you can catch more bees with a frog than you can with honey. Giving me a compassionate hug, Angela smiled through her tears and said, "The doctor will be right with you."

Dr. Frampton was new to the clinic and thus unfamiliar with my history and my bout with cancer. After a short introduction and an even quicker hand shake, he began poring over my records, which were the size of the yellow pages. He kept saying in a low authoritative voice, "Oh my God...oh my God." He continued to talk to himself as if I weren't there, and after about five minutes he turned to me, smiled and allowed me to be a part of his conversation. I have always appreciated people who talk to themselves because I somehow believe they are trying to put the pieces together while looking for answers. It's better than thinking they have some kind of mental disorder or something. I know he noticed Rad patiently sitting on Karen's lap in the corner wearing his green scrubs, sunglasses and his cancer survival hat. While he was going through the examination, I told him a few frog tales and what F.R.O.G. stood for.

After completing his look into my look sees, he wrote a prescription for meds and set up a battery of tests that would be scheduled for a later date. Dr. Frampton confided to me that his older sister was in the final stages of cancer, and she just moved to Phoenix to be closer to her family. I asked him her name and told him I'd keep her in my prayers. Next, he told me that Mary in the billing department had just gone through her daughter's bout with cancer. My next stop was Mary's office.

Mary was busy at her computer when I tapped on the side of her open door. She looked up with a smile and said, "May I help you?" I explained that Dr. Frampton had told me about her daughter and that I was also a cancer survivor. Mary invited me in like an old friend and showed me a beautiful picture of her twenty-three year old daughter before surgery to remove a cancerous tumor from behind her right eye. Even though she had lost her eye during surgery, the plastic surgeon assured her that things looked promising for reconstructive surgery.

As we were leaving the office, I told Karen it was painfully obvious that several of Rad's brother and sister frogs were needed in this office. After returning home, Karen and I prepared several of Rad's relatives for adoption. Angela's frog was about six inches high with a vest and a backpack with a tiny Velcro closure. I placed a tiny ceramic frog, that knelt with hands clasped in prayer, into the backpack and said a prayer for both her and her sister. Mary's frog for her daughter had a smile and a kiss planted on its cheek. When you squeezed him, he would respond with rib-bit, rib-bit. Dr. Frampton's frog for his sister was a small resin boot that would probably fit a two-year-old. There were two small frogs on the side of the shoe and one crawling halfway out between the tongue and the laces. Karen had made a small floral arrangement with tiny silk flowers and placed it in the boot opening.

During subsequent visits to Dr. Frampton's office, we noticed that the frogs had multiplied. There was a plethora of frogs everywhere…on top of computers, at the reception desk and in the examination rooms. It seems that the entire office was Fully Relying On God. There is always a warm reception when Rad shows up with me, and everyone is eager to show Rad his friends.

Mary's daughter's reconstructive surgery went well and she remains cancer free. Dr. Frampton's sister's quality of life was improved by a new chemotherapy plan and probably just from being around loving and caring friends and family. However, her ultimate journey attained the heights of heaven after cancer's fierce onslaught. Oh, and Angela? It seems that she has moved on to a new opportunity in her career in optometry. Life's demands are so much easier to deal with when we put our faith in God. Let go and let God.

WALKING WITH THE HOME-LESS

In late October 2007, more than a dozen wildfires threatened thousands of homes in San Diego County. The Governor declared a state of emergency in the region. Fanned by the Santa Ana winds, flames engulfed vast swaths of bone-dry southern California. More than 250,000 were forced to flee the inferno from Malibu and Santa Barbara to the suburbs of San Diego. Some managed to escape with only the clothes on their backs as the flames gobbled up 1,600 homes and businesses.

It was a cool November morning in Flagstaff as I finished packing the car to head out for the picturesque city of San Diego. My thoughts soon turned to prayers for those who lost everything and, in some cases, their lives. My services were not employed to work this catastrophe; however, Karen's were and she had preceded me. As my wife's personal Sherpa, I would bring everything needed to sustain us for the long haul. Undaunted, I pointed the car west for the nine-hour jaunt to San Diego. As my mind wandered, I wondered how I was going to amuse myself at the apartment while she worked those twelve-hour days six days a week.

I arrived in San Diego just prior to the traffic jam puzzle known as rush hour. I ran into a small glitch when I missed the turnoff for the office which was located near Qualcomm Stadium, home of the Chargers. There were seven lanes of traffic and fifty cars between me and the exit. With a considerable amount of backtracking, and my wife's tiny voice in my head saying, "Michael, you could get lost in a one-man john," I managed to locate the office. Somewhat proud of my accomplishments…that is, not making the five o'clock news, I made my way past security to

Karen's office. Karen was excited that her Sherpa had arrived with all her stuff, and I think she was glad to see me also. She rode with me to La Promenade apartments so I could unload the pachyderm/car and she could show me around a little prior to returning to work.

The apartments were located next to the trolley tracks on the Rio San Diego about a quarter mile from the office. The fall and winter weather in San Diego is nothing like Flagstaff. I found that you could wear shorts and a T-shirt and even go swimming, except for the days when the temperature would plummet all the way down into the sixties.

Karen and I began a routine where I would walk with her to work in the morning following the sidewalk next to the trolley tracks, walk her to and fro for lunch and in the evenings. During the times I wasn't walking back and forth, I would do a little reading, writing and surf the net or watch TV. I also wasn't a bad house husband…that is, doing the cooking, laundry, grocery shopping and dishes. One afternoon after lunch, Karen and I ran into one of the secretaries climbing up the stairs from the river by the trolley tracks. She said she loves to walk next to the river during her lunch hour, but warned there were many homeless along the river and would never attempt it in the evenings or after dark.

The following morning while doing a little writing, my mind kept wandering back to the previous day. I remembered our encounter with the secretary and her remarks about how beautiful it was down by the river and the homeless. I assume homeless can be a problem in large cities. The only ones I've come in contact with were in small towns like Flagstaff and when Karen and I volunteered at the soup kitchen in Wichita, Kansas. I wasn't making much progress on the book so I figured I'd amble down to the river and perhaps have a chance rendezvous with those that hang out there. I'm not intimidated by the homeless, unless they are drunk, on drugs or, in some cases, mentally ill.

I was intellectually curious about how they fared in the second largest city in California. I had inadvertently made contact with some of the homeless in the world above on street corners or in front of stores and restaurants, holding their tattered cardboard signs that read, "HOMELESS" or "HUNGRY." On one occasion, a man held his sign proudly proclaiming he was HOMELESS, HUNGRY and at the bottom of his sign, GOD. I wondered why the man didn't put God first on his list of necessities, knowing that God would take care of his need for food and shelter. Then I thought, "Why am I trying to prioritize this man's list when I have often found God at the end of mine?" I think that many of us remember a time in our lives when we believed we were only a paycheck away from being homeless ourselves.

The most profitable busy street corners, as if by virtue of right, were manned by the same person during certain hours of the day. It was as if others knew it was Tim's or Bob's corner and would not attempt to hone in on their territory and pecuniary gain. One man wearing a tattered Army fatigue shirt with PFC stripes on his shirt sleeves walked back and forth with a limp, carrying a sign promoting the fact that he was a disabled veteran. It was ironic that his favorite intersection was at the corner of the Veterans Administration building. Being a partially disabled vet myself, I knew that all this man had to do to elicit help was to walk through the front doors of that building. Karen informed me that, when one of her coworkers offered him a thirty-dollar gift certificate at a local sandwich shop, he refused. He stated, "I don't want that, all I want is cash." It's true that some of the proclaimed homeless in wealthy portions of a city may be better off than some of the working class.

As I made my way down the stairs from the world above to the one below, I could see joggers and others strolling along the path next to the river. Several of the trees and flora along the river were showing signs of autumn. The path was paved and, in some cases, completely shrouded with trees. There were concrete picnic tables sparsely placed along the route with trash receptacles next to them. I wondered what class of homeless would hang out in such a flurry of human activity. As I strolled down the path, I was surprised how clean and neat everything was. I guess I expected beer bottles, cigarette butts, abandoned clothing and sleeping bags. Instead, it was very serene and the people I passed were cordial. I thought…hey, where are the homeless, bums, tramps and vagrants? I don't know what I was expecting…maybe the scourge of the earth, but what I was about to discover could not have been further from that spectrum of humanity.

Just up the path I could see four men occupying one of the picnic tables. As I approached their table, a young female jogger paused at their table and exchanged greetings with a man she called Abraham. I slowed my pace when the four men looked up at me from their seats and Abraham the Elder motioned for me to join them. I introduced myself and Abraham acquainted me with his friends, John, Paul, and Luke.

There was nothing extraordinary about Abraham. He was medium height and build, probably in his mid- to late-sixties. His tanned brown skin, once-dark hair and his accent were proof of his Hispanic heritage. His more salt-than-pepper hair and the creases in his face testified to his age and experience. Dressed in clean, simple clothing and sporting a fresh shave, he drew me in by his demeanor. Around his neck was a leather strap securing a wallet that hung down on his chest just below his chin with a visible picture I.D. On the bench next to him was a blue backpack which held all of his worldly possessions. While we were conversing, I couldn't help but notice that his glasses were missing a lens on the right. When I inquired about it, Abraham poked his index finger under the ear piece, forward through the opening. Then waggling the finger at me, he grinned and re-marked, "Don't need it. I'm blind in this eye."

These were atypical homeless, more like the upper class of the itinerant. Yes, they were homeless, some by chance and others by choice, but they were not spiritually homeless. I didn't live with them, but as a casual observer I was allowed to see life through their street knowledge experiences. We shared stories of families and loved ones, life's challenges, God's blessings and promises. In a very short time I found that, like their names, these were in-deed God's disciples, not only for the plebeians but for those like me. Inside, I humbled myself before them, while on the outside I discussed with some pride my accomplishments. What was I doing? These men knew more about God's children and what made me tick than I would ever know. So I stayed my tongue and thoughts and decided to listen.

Abraham always sat at the same table unless it was occupied by a passing vagabond catching forty winks, at which point he would move up the river to the next available table. There were always new faces coming and going along with the familiar. Everyone on the east bank of the San Diego River knew Abraham. The east bank was lined with apartments, hotels and business complexes while the west contained restaurants, malls, shopping centers and, yes, liquor stores. Most of the lower class and some middle class in the homeless hierarchy occupied the west bank of the river. There you would find the bag ladies with their shopping carts, the dealers, addicts and disreputable. The traditional card-board beds under the trolley bridge that crosses the river and the forty-ounce empty beer bottles were scattered about.

It seemed the west bank homeless were mostly street people and had resolved defiantly that society had cast them aside. They would gather in small groups and tell stories about the day's happenings while drinking, smoking and laughing. This drinking frolic would continue until thirty minutes before the soup kitchen and shelters opened their doors. There was very little graffiti, but there were hand-written signs and symbols that the authorities allowed to remain posted indicating the direction, address and phone numbers of shelters or places food could be freely obtained.

The mentally ill and drug addicts were outcasts even in this forgotten and often-neglected society. While walking the west bank of the river, I often observed a man in a wheelchair tucked back in the pines and bushes by one of the tables. I would almost get high from his marijuana when I would stop to say, "Hello." I assumed it was for medicinal purposes for I did not know the cause or the extent of his disability. He reminded me of the "Smoking Man" in the X-files series. I thought of asking Mark (one of the undercover officers that patrol the river) about the "Smoking Man" but decided against it. I would later have a lengthy discussion with Abraham, Mark and the others about temptation, addiction and forgiveness.

Monday through Friday I would find Abraham at his table from around nine in the morning until four-thirty in the afternoon. John, Paul and Luke and some of the other regulars wouldn't show up before noon. It seems they would stop by Manpower to secure a temp job unloading trucks or as a roustabout at construction sites to pick up a few bucks and a quick trip to the unemployment office.

I enjoyed the quality one-on-one time I shared with Abraham in the mornings. Some mornings I would find him reading his tattered and worn Bible that was written in Spanish. The pages were dog-eared and torn and just about everything in his Bible was either underlined or circled and the margins were full of notes. I then thought about my Bible…it looks brand-new and that's not good for my soul. There is so much I must learn from this man, but first…who is he?

I asked Abraham if he wouldn't mind answering a personal question. "No, what is it?" "Have you ever been arrested?" He paused for a moment, smiled and responded, "other than for urinating in public and indecent exposure…Yes." He went on to say that he and his girlfriend immigrated to San Antonio, Texas when he was seventeen and she was sixteen. She found work as a maid at the hotel where they were staying and he was a day laborer. Shortly after their arrival, Abraham turned eighteen and the hotel owner reported him to the authorities. He was arrested for statutory rape and thrown behind bars. He said they had been childhood sweethearts and age never crossed their minds. With help from his parents in Mexico and monies he had saved, he obtained a good lawyer and after three months in jail, he was cleared of all charges. His girlfriend refused to press charges and because of her age, was deported to Mexico and Abraham became a U.S. citizen.

Abraham told me that his wife convinced him to give up drinking over twenty years ago. "She sounds like a fine woman…that is, to persuade you to give up something as addictive as alcohol." He went on to say that his addiction had reached the point that he would go out every night and get drunk.

"So how did your wife persuade you to give it up?" I asked.

"Well," Abraham responded, "after an all-night binge with one of my drinking buddies, I made my way home in the wee hours and found myself sitting on the toilet contemplating my navel while waiting for the room to stop spinning. I sobered up quickly when my wife entered the bathroom accusing me of infidelity while pointing my thirty-eight special at my head."

"Wow! What did you do?"

"What could I do with my pants down around my ankles, sitting on the john, looking down the barrel of my Smith & Wesson? I pleaded with her. I convinced her that I was out with my buddy, Jose, and she could call him if she wanted to verify that I was telling the truth."

"So you haven't had a drink since?"

Abraham admitted that he would partake in a celebratory glass of wine with those who are fortunate enough to land a full-time job.

"Where is your wife now?"

"Probably back in San Antonio. I avoid her like the plague."

Abraham was homeless by choice. He worked at a steady job long enough to receive Social Security benefits, though I don't think he had a retirement. A self-sufficient man, he found the outdoors not as confining as the four walls of his apartment. So Abraham gave away all his possessions to the poor. He was neither proud nor arrogant. Rather, he was very meek but strong in the convictions of his faith. He told me that the walls closed in on him, forcing him to the streets. I believe that this is where God wanted His child to be. He told me that this earth, with all the pain and suffering, is so beautiful that he can't imagine the abode of God. I believe that Abraham's command of the English language was comparable to mine, though he preferred to read in Spanish.

I asked Abraham, "Where do you sleep?"

"On the trolleys," he acknowledged.

"How can you sleep with the trolleys signaling their departure after every stop?"

"Like a baby," he responded. "It kind of rocks me to sleep until they kick us off at the one a.m. turnaround."

"What do you do then?"

"I walk across the tracks and board the south-bound train."

He went on to tell me that he had a senior citizen pass that allows him to ride all day and night if he wanted. "

"Why do you sleep on the trolley?"

"It's clean, warm and safe. Besides you meet a lot of wonderful people on the trolley."

"What about your parents?" I asked.

"Though I left home at an early age, I visited with them often, and in sixty-three years of marriage, to my knowledge, they never argued."

"Where are they now?"

"They are with our Lord, both died in their sleep as if the Lord ushered them both to heaven."

The following is one of many conversations that took place at Abraham's table with John, Paul, Luke and Mark. These are their real first names and, yes, they are disciples of Christ. As in most of our discussions, others walking down the east river path would gather around Abraham's table to listen. His Bible was always close by, though he seldom read to us from it. On this day, Abraham's teachings were about temptations, addictions and forgiveness.

Abraham: Addiction comes in many forms from drugs, sex, and wealth to self-importance. It begins innocent enough with temptation. The first cigarette makes you sick but the last does not have to seal your fate. Each time we allow Satan to direct our hands with his suggestions, they become our needs, wants and desires and he wins. To resist temptation, build a wall against sin. Another "fix" fuels the fires of hell. Remember, every life touches another.

Luke: God gave us his Son Jesus Christ born of the flesh and weak with desires. Jesus was tempted many times by trials and tribulations and taught us how to resist the call of Satan.

Mark: Do you think it would be easier to resist temptation and avoid addiction if you were fully aware of the consequences of your choices?

Paul: Jesus' life was ministered by angels under the watchful eye of His Father's never-ending presence. Was it a burden knowing there would be millions of books and thousands of movies portraying His life, teachings and death while on earth?

Abraham: The true unfathomable burden was to gather our sins onto Him and to die with them so we don't have to. As I said before, every life touches another and the weight of just one of our sins can be more than we can bear.

John: Can you imagine a loving father holding his drunken son or absorbing some of the pain and anger from a daughter on crystal meth?

Mark: Sharing your pain and suffering with others who love you opens life's angry door to understanding and forgiveness.

Luke: We may be helpless fighting the demons alone, but with the help of angels and the blood of Christ, they are lifted from our soul. The first step to forgiveness is to ask.

Abraham: When one man cannot lift the stone by himself, he employs others to assist. If a task is insurmountable by himself, he may employ the help of others to budge the stone; though it may be of a great burden to all.

A voice from the gathering: What about envy?

Abraham: Envy isn't alluring because it's the only vice without a reward! Envious people are coreless, because they drink too much to escape boredom. Believe me, I speak from experience. Faith is not a game. But if you practice faith in everything you do, you win the love of your Creator and if you don't, Satan wins. This is not a win-win situation and eternity is an awful long time to be at a dead-end job serving Lucifer.

"The Scripture, foreseeing that God would justify the Gentiles by faith, preached the gospel beforehand to Abraham, saying, 'ALL THE NATIONS WILL BE BLESSED IN YOU.'" Galatians 3:8

As weeks passed, it became obvious a position would not become available to work in the office with Karen. That was just as well, for I was Abraham's student and there was much to learn before I could be a teacher. Abraham's first lesson to me was self-importance and pride. *"When pride comes, then comes dishonor, But with the humble is wisdom."* Proverbs 11:2

The following months, the word passed throughout Karen's office that my unemployed time was spent with the homeless by the river. Some of Karen's cohorts. though well-meaning, would ask such questions as, "Are you still hanging out with the homeless?" or "Aren't you scared of them?"

I would just smile and reply "Yes, they are homeless and some are even helpless, but none of them are hopeless."

One afternoon while walking with Karen back to the apartment for lunch, Karen turned to me with a gracious smile and in a faint, mincing voice said, "Michael, you don't have a life." When I asked her what she meant by that, she replied, "I mean you spent the last four months with homeless people."

I smiled and continued holding her hand until we reached the trolley station. There I escorted her down the stairs to the world below on the banks of the San Diego River. Karen had walked with me before on both sides of the river. She had even seen the "Smoking Man" and the basket people, but she had never met Abraham. As we approached Abraham's table, John, Paul, Luke and Mark stood up in a courteous acknowledgement as Abraham extended a warm greeting. After a short introduction and cordial reception, Karen and I excused ourselves and bid them farewell.

After we ascended the stairs to the world above, Karen turned to me and said, "Michael, you do have a life and I'm glad that I am a part of it."

Karen was given a release date from the catastrophe operation about four months after her arrival. I began to pack some things around the apartment in preparation for our departure. I kept wondering about Abraham and how to tell him that we were leaving. When I approached his table, it was as if he already knew.

The first words out of his mouth were, "Michael, I will see you and be with you again at the Lord's table. This is not goodbye but rather Godspeed, for we will break bread together, we will glorify our Father together for all eternity."

I told Abraham that Karen wanted to see him before we left. He said he had a dentist appointment in the morning but would try to be at the table after two. As I departed his company, I somehow knew this would be the last time I would see him. The following afternoon, Karen and I made several trips to Abraham's empty table. That night I thought of Abraham every time a trolley passed the apartments. Good night, my brother…Godspeed.

Red, White and Blue

It was Christmas Eve and I was sitting with Wayne, an old friend and neighbor of fifteen years. Two heart attacks and innumerable strokes had taken their toll on Wayne's mind, body and eyesight. I had told his wife, Edna, that I would stay with him while she went to the Christmas Eve service with my wife, Karen. Wayne appeared noticeably confused and his speech was somewhat impaired. After reading to him from the Bible for awhile, I asked, "Wayne, do you know who I am?"

He responded, "I…I think you're a friend."

I inquired further, "Do you know what day it is?"

He shook his head no.

"It's Christmas Eve, Wayne."

His face lit up like a child's. Stuttering he said, "It's Jesus'....
Jesus'..." I helped him with the word "birthday."

As we continued to converse, I found that his memory of the
distant past, although fragmented, was the best place to sojourn.

Wayne told me, "I always loved singing. When Edna was younger, she would sing in the choir at church and around the house."
He paused thoughtfully. "I used to love to sing, too. But one of
my aunts made fun of my singing. That ruined it for me."

Glancing in my direction, he commented, "You know I can't see
you."

I responded, "You can hear me, can't you?"

Wayne responded affirmatively and proceeded to tell me, "You
know, a good woman is hard to find. Edna's a good woman. I
would perish if it weren't for Edna."

He became silent and appeared to be in deep thought, trying to
grasp what he wanted to say or how he wanted to say it. With
five words, Wayne tugged at my heart strings saying, "Jesus will
sing for me."

I began to cry as I thought about Jesus dying for us. Why
wouldn't He sing for his Father's children? Yes, Wayne, Jesus will
sing for you.

May 30th, Memorial Day, originally called Decoration Day, is a
day of remembrance for those who died in service to our nation.
Edna Winters awoke that morning next to a man who didn't
recognize her after a 66-year covenant. At first, Wayne thought
Edna was his brother and then let out a scream as the last very
fine cord of reality snapped. Undaunted, Edna loaded Wayne in

the truck and headed off to the cemetery where she would rake, clean, place flowers at the graves of soldiers and kneel before the fallen. Wayne sat in the truck, oblivious to the work and prayers that Edna now shouldered alone. Her mind must have been reeling as she labored under her burdens.

I was standing next to the driveway when Edna returned with her precious cargo. While helping her with Wayne, I realized he was with our Father and our Father was with her. I didn't realize that Edna knew I was praying until she stopped me and said, "I know what you're doing. You're praying." Yes, I was doing what the Lord asked of me two years ago when he grabbed me by the arm and said, "I have work for you to do."

As I looked out the upstairs window, I saw the red, white and blue colors flying in front of the Winters' home, a memorial to soldiers lost but not forgotten. I had promised Edna I would help her with some chores that day and, yes, I would pray.

In 1932, Mary Elizabeth Frye wrote:
> Do not stand at my grave and weep,
> I am not there; I do not sleep.
> I am a thousand winds that blow,
> I am the diamond glints on snow,
> I am the sun on the ripened grain,
> I am the gentle autumn rain.
> When you awaken in the morning's hush,
> I am the swift uplifting rush
> Of quiet birds in circled flight.
> I am the soft stars that shine at night.
> Do not stand at my grave and cry,
> I am not there; I did not die."

"Fight the good fight of faith; take hold of the eternal life to which you were called, and you made the good confession in the presence of many witnesses." 1 Timothy 6:12

When the autumn colors blazed and the leaves began to fall, it was apparent to me that Wayne's health was declining further. He continued to have mild strokes and heart attacks and suffer from delusions and hallucinations. Wayne was almost completely helpless and was barely able to walk with assistance. Edna and I have talked many times, and she is so thankful that Wayne had asked to be baptized …and he was at the young age of eighty-eight.

Edna took her wedding vows seriously and lived by the covenant made with this man "in sickness and in health, as long as we both shall live." One day, Wayne just lay down on the kitchen floor and Edna wasn't able to get him up. She began calling everyone on her "list" to no avail. There he stayed for almost an hour until Karen and I returned home and saw that Edna had attempted to contact us. Hospice helped at their home with bathing and other needs, but I was sure Edna was afraid that the time would come when she would have to turn over Wayne's complete care to the inpatient hospice facility.

Every week after the early church service I contacted Edna to see if she would like for me to stay with Wayne while she attended a later service. Since I cared for Wayne every other week or so, I noticed his deterioration more so than Edna who was with him constantly. Her unswerving love and devotion to this man was unfathomable. Sure, she was human and often told me if it weren't for Jesus she didn't know how she would do it. What a void there must be for those that do not have faith in the Lord during trials and life's tribulations.

Wayne's dementia had progressed to the point that he was no longer oriented and a conversation was limited to less than a handful of words. Another Sunday as I stayed with him while Edna was in church, I was reading the Bible to Wayne. He asked me, "Are you yawning?"

Taking a swig from my water bottle I admitted, "Yes, you caught me yawning."

"So what's that you're drinkin'?," he posed. "Whiskey?"

Startled I asked, "Can you see me?"

Wayne nodded. Then, just when I thought there were no surprises left in this man, he leaned forward in his chair and affirmed, "I know who you are. Your name is Michael and cancer saved your soul." The Wayne I knew was slowly leaving his body but the Jesus I know was with his soul.

Several months after I wrote this part of the book, Wayne left to be with his heavenly Father. He passed away in his sleep, in his own bed sometime after Edna had kissed him on the forehead. Be at rest, Wayne. I know that Jesus is singing for you.

PART 4

SPIRITUAL MUSINGS

Spiritual Modality

I have come to believe that God blesses some with divine gifts in the hours just prior to their death. The mental side of this phenomenon can be divine insight, which gives foreknowledge of things to come, or hindsight, which reveals previously hidden past events, and melds them with the known to create clarity and understanding within relationships. The physical side can be return of health, speech, or the sense of sight. I believe most children of God will experience this rapture and speak with knowledge not known to most mortals.

My Dad

I saw this for the first time with my father. He suffered a stroke which caused his speech to be slurred and the left side of his body to be partially paralyzed during the last few years of his life. Then one day my sister called to tell me Pop was in the hospital and he wasn't doing very well. I called the hospital and got through to the ward my father was on. When they rang his room, to my surprise, he answered the phone. His speech was so slurred that I couldn't understand him.

It's a twenty-two-hour drive from Flagstaff, Arizona to Houston, Texas. But I knew my father was dying and in desperation, I told him that I could leave that day, drive straight through and be there with him the next afternoon. In a crisp, clear, deep voice my father said, "SON THAT WILL NOT BE NECESSARY." Wow! I just about dropped the phone. It had been very difficult to understand Pop since his second stroke. I asked myself, "Was this really my father talking?"

But then, in this clear, strong voice, he proceeded to tell me how proud he was of me for the work I did for the Department of Defense Special Projects Division. My father had no prior knowledge of my work since most of it was classified. However, he seemed to know things that I have never told anyone. I was speechless. Finally, he told me that he loved me and said good-bye. But this "goodbye" was more a blessing as "God be with you" or "godbwye."

The next morning while we were at church, I told my wife Karen that my father had just died. I felt his spirit departing. When we got home, there was a message from my sister on the answering machine.

HOMETOWN HARDWARE

There is a hardware store in our little mountain town that encourages its employees to talk about spiritual things, preach the gospel and glorify God. I bet you didn't know a hardware store like that existed. When you go in there, you'll leave with much more than a 2x4 or a sack of nails. You can get a free dose of the Holy Spirit. Don't worry, this doesn't mean they pounce on you when you come through the door and thump the Bible at you. It's more like them sharing stories about their walk in faith and you can share yours.

I told Jack at the store about the loss of my father...what he had said and how he said it...just before he died. Jack told me that his mother, Ann, had been living with them after she lost her sight five years earlier. He and his mother were sitting in the living room, Ann in her favorite chair and he in his. Jack was reading the newspaper and had just started to read the comic section, when his mother asked him to put down the comics and come to her. As he had said, she was blind. But Jack figured she must have heard the rustling of the paper as he turned the pages. When he approached her, she reached up grabbed his hands and smiled as she touched his face with her eyes. Then Jack's wife entered the room. His mother turned to her and exclaimed what a beautiful dress she had on and began to describe it.

Jack and his wife realized this was more than extrasensory perception; her sight had returned. Ann rejoiced with her family and began to cry out in exaltation to the Lord God. Jack didn't know his mother was being called home. All three were praying and glorifying Christ Jesus when a massive heart attack took Ann from them and into the arms of God.

I told Jack that my eyes were open and I could see, and yet I was blind to the Holy Spirit. If He hadn't found me, I would still be stumbling over my meager belief in Alpha and Omega and my pitiful self.

Jack told me it has been over thirty-four years since he had given himself to Christ. He said he was sitting in church with his fiancée when he was called during the sermon. Jack didn't recall what the sermon was about. All he knew was Christ called out to him. (Our Father calls to all of us, but do you turn a deaf, soulless ear towards firmament?)

At the end of the sermon, the preacher asked those who desired to give themselves to the Lord to come forward. As Jack began to stand up, his fiancée grabbed his arm and pulled his ear towards her lips and whispered urgently, "Sit down! Don't embarrass me!"

Jack replied, "I can't help it. I have to go." He had been called by the Lord and he was offering himself to His services.

After he had accepted Christ Jesus as his Lord and Savior, Jack stood with the pastor in a receiving line as the congregation greeted and welcomed him. Jack's soon-to-be bride was in line also, but she was sobbing. She asked Jack, "Can you ever forgive me for trying to hold you back?"

Jack just put his arms around her and held her saying, "It wasn't you that tried to keep me from the Lord; it was Satan." "...*[if]* *My people who are called by My name humble themselves and pray and seek My face and turn from their wicked ways, then I will hear from heaven, will forgive their sin and will heal their land." 2 Chronicles 7:14*

PRAYER WALK

May 3, 2006 was the National Day of Prayer. I was at the main Hospital in Flagstaff, not as a patient this time, but one of several who had come to pray. I met with others that morning and we broke into two groups of three and began a prayerful walk through the halls and wards at the hospital. With reverence, we bowed our heads as though we were in a cathedral. A hospital has the grandeur of all churches and faiths culminated as one. Most of us were born in one and will die in one. Charged with the joy at the arrival of a newborn or the sorrow at the loss of a loved one, prayers flow like the river of life down the halls and through its doors. Prayers offered to our Lord Almighty are His and can never be disavowed.

Prayer walking and pausing at various places to gather my thoughts for the patients, doctors, nurses and staff throughout this basilica, I became mindful of the disembodied spirits of the deceased; I could see the umbra and feel the phantom of souls. I asked the Holy Spirit, "Cleanse the buildings from all evil and wickedness. Drive out Satan and the fear he engenders. Through Your power, bring calming warmth and the presence of our Lord to permeate the buildings. May the grounds become holy and may angels greet everyone at the door."

While we were praying in the halls of the in-patient wards, a woman came out of one of the rooms and asked, "Are you praying?"

Deeply in prayer, we were caught off guard by her approach. I responded, "Were we that obvious?"

"Would you please come pray over my mother?" she asked, leading us to the side of a woman who appeared to be suffering from advanced Alzheimer's. As we entered the room, I could feel the power of the Holy Spirit and the presence of angels. This gray-haired child of God was lying on her side facing her son-in-law, Craig, who was on the phone attempting to arrange full-time care for her. We prayerfully gathered at the foot of her bed. Then, one by one, we went to her side, held her hand and caressed her forehead.

As I approached her, I noticed that she was drooling and mumbling an unintelligible word salad. As I clasped her hand and gently caressed her forehead, she turned with a jerk and stared into my eyes and began to speak. "My son-in-law, Craig, has been very good to me. He prepared a place in his garden where I could go to pray and talk with the Lord." She continued speaking quite clearly. She confessed that she hadn't been one of the faithful in her youth but that she had eventually come to know her Lord and Savior. She affirmed her confidence that He had prepared a place for her in Heaven.

Craig stopped in the middle of his phone conversation. Startled, he stared and began to listen to his mother-in-law, who was now a very lucid woman. I was praying, listening, and learning about her salvation through Christ's blood and her obedience to God. Suddenly, just as quickly as she had turned toward me, she turned away and slipped back down into the fog of her illness.

A close friend of mine was part of the prayer team on that day. He has often told me that the lessons and blessings we receive from others far outnumber anything we can give. My heart was humbled by this woman's discipleship and her faith in the Lord. For the rest of the day I pondered the insights I had received during that woman's transport into brief clarity.

The next day I asked my friend about this and he explained that many things are made known to us as they were with my father prior to his death. Working with the chaplain's office at the hospital, I'm sure he has seen this many times. I imagine most of us will experience this unless we're hit by a bus or train. As for me, I plan to go to sleep and wake up in heaven. *(If you want to hear God laugh, tell him what YOUR plans are.)*

ALBERT

While visiting my wife, Karen, who was on temporary assignment in Springfield, Missouri, I stopped in Wal-Mart to pick up a few items. There I stood in front of the milk cooler contemplating a major decision for a retired person, "Should I get a gallon of one-percent or two-percent milk?" While in deep thought or deep in a senior moment, I heard a voice.

"When I was on the farm, we drank what came straight from the cow." I looked up and there he was, a servant of God pushing a cart full of tools. His name tag told me his name was "Albert." This toothless, rugged, seventy-two-year-old man's face was wreathed with wrinkles and lit by a warm smile. As we began to exchange stories about life on the farm, I felt as if I was in the presence of God's messenger. Angels are God's police force and are sent to serve and protect. As servants of the Lord, they do not judge nor ask what sins these souls may have committed.

Albert told me that he had lost his wife, Mary, to Alzheimer's and heart disease two years before. Her condition had progressed from senile dementia to loss of speech and sight altogether. Towards the end, Albert said he was praying over Mary when her cognitive processes returned along with her sight. He related that Mary had started talking about the Rapture and how Jesus Christ would descend from heaven with the onset of the Great Tribulation. Albert said Mary went from ecstasy to tranquility and finally to total peace as she passed on while he held her in his arms. I placed my hands on Albert's shoulders and he placed his on mine as we began to pray right in front of the milk coolers at Wal-mart.

As we were discussing our faith and inevitable destiny with the Lord, Albert's walky-talky went off. "Albert…Albert where are you?" Albert told me that he hopes he lives long enough to see the Great Tribulation. He went on to say, "Can't you just see the ceiling of the store opening up as Jesus descends. I have nothing to lose and everything to gain."

I responded, "Stop it, Albert. You're scaring me. Besides, I would hope I'd be leaving with the first bunch, if I'm here for the Rapture." As his walky-talky went off for the third time, I told him, "It's been great to talk to you, but maybe you ought to answer that. I don't want to get you in trouble."

In a stern, almost reprimanding voice Albert responded to me, "I fear what no man can do to my body. But I do fear the one that can take my soul" (I later learned his words were from Luke 12:4-5). Then he bid me farewell as he reached for his walky-talky while pushing his basket of tools down the aisle.

At the checkout stand, I asked the cashier what she thought about Albert. She smiled, "We all just love him." I couldn't imagine how anyone wouldn't love him.

Musings

As I have mentioned, I frequently prayed for guidance as I was writing about my journey. The Holy Spirit always came through, although not always as quickly as my impatient heart would have liked. Still, the story flowed along smoothly. Occasionally, however, my prayer for inspiration would result in a need to write about topics that didn't quite fit into the chronology of the story. I wrote about them anyway (you don't reject a gift from the Holy Spirit). These musings were like eddies on the side of a gushing stream; they were composed of the same spiritual water as the stream, but were not a part of the main current.

Several of these are included as part of this section.

Wind Chimes

For Christmas one year, my mother bought every man, woman and child in our family a "bird clock." It seems she fell in love with the hourly songs of the mourning dove, the house finch and robin. As far as I was concerned, these sounds belonged outside not inside my house. However, I placed the clock on the wall in the solarium which was somewhat removed from the rest of our home and hoped the batteries would give out soon.

Two years later I wanted to strangle the Energizer Bunny inside this demonic clock. I still couldn't put the thing to rest because I remembered how much my mother loved it and wanted to share with us. When my sister told me that her clock had finally given up the ghost, I knew there was some hope.

The one redeeming factor was the clock remained mute from sunset to sunrise and, like screaming kids, after a while you learn to ignore it. Occasionally a visitor would exclaim, "What is that ungodly sound coming from your solarium?"

After the passing of my mother, the batteries in the clock also began to wind down. I was somehow saddened that the chickadee now sounded more like a dying duck in a thunderstorm. It was a matter of days before the clock warbled its last notes. However, this clock now stirred up sentiments of my mother's bright consciousness. I had to replace the batteries. As I did so, I thought, "This should keep alive the phantom memories of my mother's spirit." I now listen for her spirit in the hourly songs of the clock.

Inspired by the auditory remembrance the bird clock provided, Karen suggested that we create a musical reminder of other departed loved ones by placing dedicated wind chimes in the various trees of our yard. Strategically placed in harmonious relationship with the wind, the chimes create a tuneful melody like cheerful words whispered. Karen and I set out on a quest to find chimes, some decorated with colorful ceramics, twinkling stained glass, metal or wood, and a peaceful concord of sounds corresponding to our memories of departed loved ones. It wasn't morbid like selecting a gravestone but rather it was exciting to find the perfect wind chime that brought strong feelings of joy and remembrance.

Over a period of time we were able to acquire chimes in memory of our parents, families and loved ones. Karen even managed to find a wind chime depicting two kitties which we hung in memory of Axel and Raistlin. High in the Dutch Elm tree in the backyard hangs a five foot tubular chime somewhat shielded from the strong winds by the tree branches. We had given it to a neighbor. He and his wife had become like family to us. When she passed away, he sold their house and moved, giving us the wind chime we had given to them as a remembrance. On a blustery day it is like a cathedral carillon, sounding peaceful tones and recreating heartfelt impressions of the dear ones who have left our lives but not our hearts. On a calm day the chimes rest but when touched by a hand, they will articulate harmonies that evoke deep emotions.

When I became ill with cancer, I tried but couldn't envision the look and sound of my wind chime...I now know why. Like Gabriel, with trumpet raised and facing east ready to proclaim the second coming of Christ, I am here to proclaim the Lord with breath and words guided by the Holy Spirit...not a whisper in the wind.

A Quiet Place

Eric, my son, was angry about something and out of the blue he said in a fulminating voice, "My dad speaks to God!" I corrected him and told him, "No – I pray to God." Insistent, he replied, "My dad talks with God."

A conversation with the Lord is not one-sided. If you don't get an answer to your prayers, it doesn't mean that He's not listening

– on the contrary, He is a very good listener…are you listening? When I have prayed long and hard for something but I didn't get an answer, I thought that was the answer – "no." Does the expression, "You have been the answer to my prayers," or "You have been a godsend," say anything to you? The Holy Spirit has used me many times as a conduit of His messages. When you say, "Here I am Lord," be mindful. He'll take you up on that.

I find that it's a lot easier for me to talk with God in a quiet place such as a church or alone in a field of flowers as opposed to a traffic jam. While mowing the lawn, I sometimes pray. Mowing the lawn is like being in a quiet place because all other sounds are muffled with the roar of the lawn mower. As I was mowing and thanking the Holy Spirit for all the blessings He has bestowed upon me, He said, "I am the reason you lost the lead role in the movie directed by Satan – that's right, Lucifer himself."

Not knowing what kind of mind game I was involved in, I asked a stupid question. "What is the name of this movie?"

"From Eternity to Hell."

Going along with this, I was now curious, "So what part did I try out for?"

"The one you rehearsed for most of your life: DEAD CHRISTIAN WALKING."

I've found that God has a sense of humor and He does smile upon His children. Was the Lord playing with His child or do I have an overactive imagination? I don't know, but I don't think I could have thought up this bizarre but rather humorous scene.

Covenant

A family, like a marriage, is a lifelong commitment and is made of many persons and kinships. Most couples are capable of making babies, but that in itself does not make you a family or give you the blessed privilege of being referred to as Mom and Dad. The trust and love parents receive from their offspring is earned through a mutual family setting. A father and a mother are nothing more than seed donors. An adopted child is not of your blood but is like any child desiring love and the sanctity found within the family. When a son or daughter attempts to emulate their parents, that's when true bonding begins. The privilege of being called Mom or Dad comes through a parent's teachings of right from wrong, good from bad or through just being there for a child that is hurt, scared or confused.

Being a parent is a huge responsibility and the child must come first during its formative years. Selfishness and self-centeredness do not make for a strong cohesion in a family unit. What binds a family together? Love and trust. It's knowing that someone will be there to catch you if you stumble and fall or hold you when life crushes your emotions and feelings. A grounding source for any child is the alliance or bond between parents. A relationship is not a give and take proposition. There is no individual scoring, only a team effort. There is no room for tit for tat or a volley of repartee...I did this and you did that. In most cases the score keeper has little interest in the game, only the scoreboard. A relationship/family is not about you, me or the children. It's about us, the unity of one. When you cut, I bleed.

Creating a strong and meaningful relationship is like being a sharecropper. The ground you work belongs to the union and each of you shares the fruit of your labors with those you love. The two of you start out together and begin to cultivate the union of man and woman. It's a small plot of land with a few weeds and rocks here and there but together, the land is cleared and the soil is prepared for the seeds of life. You plant, fertilize and water the seeds and hold one another close while smiling upon your labors. The small plot of land has grown into a family garden. Be diligent, for weeds will sprout among the fruit and destructive forces outside your garden may attempt to enter. All too often a stranger is allowed in your garden to partake of the fruits of your labors. An early frost in a marriage can have devastating effects. That is not the time to go in search of another plot of land to start over. The next one you find may have more weeds and rocks than the first and the soil could be barren. When life's storms come…and they will – join together, spread your arms and protect all that God has provided you. A stormy relationship may severely damage all that you both have worked to create.

Don't allow yourselves to fall out of love. Thank goodness a marriage is warming rather than an inferno, consuming everything around it, for that is known as lust. Keep the home fires burning with kisses, compliments and flowers. Twenty-four years ago Karen was a manager for a local phone company. When they eliminated her position, she was let go. Devastated, she called me in tears and asked me to come and help her gather her belongings. I showed up with a nosegay of flowers and a handful of boxes to assist her with her things. It turned out God had future plans for her with a reputable company with a 401K, health plan, and retirement program.

Through our forty years of marriage we have weathered many a storm together. Someone once asked me how many years we have been together. Jokingly I responded, "Let me put it this way, I don't look both ways when I cross the street anymore." With that remark, I got a corresponding jab from an elbow to my ribs. Holding my side, I turned to my wife and best friend and she just smiled. That's right. I called Karen my best friend. If you really love someone, you also know what buttons to push to hurt them. Love can turn to hate in a heartbeat. Thus, a marriage must not be based solely on love alone. If the person that you love is also your best friend, you'll be there for them even if they strike out at you in anger.

Karen has been my best friend for over fifty years. In the seventh grade I sat behind her and pulled her hair to get her attention. It worked. She invited me to the seventh-grade picnic. Childhood sweethearts, we went to the prom together and on to college. I took French my first year and hated every minute of it. I would sit in French class and think about the girl of my dreams. So much so, I started cutting my class in order to sit with Karen in her history class. Her professor must have thought I was an auditor for he would call the roll and stare at me. Her teacher came off like a geeky nerd who spoke with a high lisping voice. I can still hear him saying, "The Egyptians were very earthy people." Thank God I loved that woman because my French class was starting to look better all the time.

Wedding vows are a serious covenant made between two people willing to share their lives with one another. You can't just honor part of the contract and cross out the parts you don't like. A marriage can't be special-ordered by leaving out the parts with which you don't want to deal (e.g., better or worse, richer or poorer, sickness and in health). Marriage is about sharing, not separating the wheat from the chaff. There should be very little room in a relationship for the "M" word. This is MY house, MY car, MY money. Even as adults it's hard to share and use the word OUR. We don't hesitate to use the word YOUR for things or duties we don't want to share. You need to clean up after YOUR dog or all the stuff in the messy garage is YOURS! On the other hand, the word "I" is very apropos in a healthy relationship. I need some time to think about it or I need to be alone for a while.

My son, Eric, told me that a friend had confided in him that he had fallen in love with a special young lady and was thinking of asking her hand in marriage. How does one know if they're in love or infatuated with being in love? Eric had to pull only one word out of the marriage covenant -"sickness." He asked his friend if he would be willing in his old age to feed and diaper this person if needed.

Infatuation can fly right out love's window in the face of reality. The thought of growing old together may seem romantic, but with all things in life there is a price. The thought of being a solitary traveler through life, companionless, alone without the memories and comfort of family and friends is sad. Some fall in love with themselves. Still, not liking what they see in the mirror may cause them to spend many lonesome hours in bars searching. Once you realize you're a good person and willing to share your love with others, you know there is someone for everyone...even you.

The sun came up this morning. Did you notice? While wiping the sleep from my eyes I realized, it's Saturday. I'm off! Not just another day, a day off! Great! I didn't plan again. It kind of snuck up on me. While laying in a sleepy stupor I thought, "Get up, grab your wife, call your family to your side and tell them that you love them. Take life's precious time and use it wisely. Let the world spin without you and your family for a few minutes. The housework, dirty laundry and bills can wait while you wrap your arms around all the love a family and friends have to offer in life." I thought, "I should have done this yesterday and the day before that."

There is too much negatively charged electricity in life. Fortunately, electricity flows from negative to positive. Use that power to banish the gloom of darkness. Illuminate life's shadows with cheerfulness and buoyant spirits. Every day is a gift and with

God's help, I plan to use my gifts sagaciously and ignore the low-down moments a day at a time.

LETTER TO MY TEACHER

Dear Teacher,

The spiritually-wise mentor who listens with understanding, can and will learn from the student being taught. If nothing else, learn who I am and what I seek from you. Your humility is a wonderful trait. Don't sacrifice it to lack of patience or become frustrated and annoyed with me if I am overzealous or appear to be suffering from egotism or pride. *"The righteous cry, and the LORD hears And delivers them out of all their troubles. The LORD is near to the brokenhearted And saves those who are crushed in spirit." Psalm 34:17-18*

The Bible teaches us to go about our work as though we are working for the Lord. *"Whatever you do, do your work heartily, as for the Lord rather than for men." Colossians 3:23* How can I look on the fruits of my labor and remain humble, and contain my enthusiasm? It's not pride that fans the flame of my heart. It is joy and gratitude for what God has done for me and through me. *"Let your light shine before men in such a way that they may see your good works, and glorify your Father who is in heaven." Matthew 5:16*

How can I calmly "tell it on the mountain" when my spirit is aching to shout to the world that Jesus has blessed me and is the Lord of my life? *"Then I heard the voice of the Lord saying, 'Whom shall I send, and who will go for us?' Then I said, 'Here am I, send me!' " Isaiah 6:8* Please don't judge me as vain. My jubilance in my newly discovered discipleship might be misinterpreted as pride. But the wise mentor delineates pride from passion and does not condemn or criticize. Surely you know that God's grace does not bestow theological virtue to a prideful man. Don't confuse my eagerness with arrogance when I turn to you for counsel. I long for you to encourage me with your strong example, remaining calm and focused. Guide me, for though you think me blind, I may see farther than you think. Try to see what I see.

Perhaps you didn't think that you were my teacher or don't want to be my teacher. Life's lesson never ends. In fact, life is itself a great endless lesson. There is always something to learn or someone to teach. When we fail at one or the other, there is still the "school of hard knocks" and the lesson is taught whether we wanted it or not. My struggle with cancer left me with a great thirst. Not a physical thirst, but the thirst that only Christ can quench. You showed me your knowledge and shared the living water with me. Wasn't it you who said, "Knowledge comes with power," and that "Power is dangerous unless you have the wisdom to apply it and know of the consequences"? Be careful of your authority and influence over your student. Turn to prayer for guidance. God will give you the wisdom to deal with me. Wisdom is one of God's kisses, for true wisdom comes through and from the grace of God.

You taught me to disciple myself first before raining knowledge down on others. My soul is childlike, curious, and ready to learn new things and reexamine lessons taught. *"Teach me, and I will be silent; And show me how I have erred. How painful are honest words! But what does your argument prove? Do you intend to reprove my words, When the words of one in despair belong to the wind?" Job 6:24-26* Have you remembered to make room in your heart for my love and friendship? As your pupil, I long to confide in you. *"A pupil is not above his teacher; but everyone, after he has been fully trained, will be like his teacher." Luke 6:40* Understand individuality and treat your student as an equal. Learn to accept the point of view of others and avoid being judgmental. With God-given ability, examine the whole person and avoid concentrating only on the soul. Remain strong in your convictions, but spiritually modest for the Lord knows all about you and He still loves you as He does me.

I have many questions and there are many spiritual battles to be fought for our soul, so I'll begin with temptation. God gave us a living choice, a way out either by calling on the name of the Lord or an escape route to eternal life through a gift to us…His Son, Christ Jesus. *"Behold, I stand at the door and knock; if anyone hears My voice and opens the door, I will come in to him and will dine with him, and he with Me." Revelation 3:20* Satan is relentless, but by inviting the Lord into my heart, I slam the door on Satan and he will depart from me. I remain vigilant through prayer, for I know he will return at a more opportune time when I am weaker. *"Keep watching and praying that you may not enter into temptation; the spirit is willing, but the flesh is weak." Matthew 26:41*

Teachers are angels' helpers by their ministries and guidance. If we do not know God, we are quickly snared and enslaved by our trespasses. Teacher, be wary, for only angels can "trespass *quare clausum fregit*" (the defendant unlawfully enters the land of the plaintiff). In other words, to transgress Satan's boundaries is to stand in his path, defying him on his ground in the skies above and the depths below. If we as mortals attempt this, we may be blinded by Satan and ultimately lose this battle. I am but a human and even though my spirit is guided by heaven's hand, I stumble like a child and fall in His hallowed footprints. Counselor, the path is narrow, walk with me so I will not stray. I would rather spend my life close to the bird rather than wasting it wishing I had wings.

Teacher, my conscience is an awesome gift from God that allows me to examine my inner self and permits me to be cognizant rather than oblivious to my faults and misgivings towards others. If allowed, my conscience creates remorse, provides moral and spiritual guidance and internal knowledge of oneself. It is neither a mirage nor an illusion, rather a window to my inner person that creates an outward expression. Moral dualism is a philosophy of mind, a chaotic haze where a plethora of conflicts between good and evil takes place. A guilty conscience is relieved with forgiveness and cleansed through prayer. Does that mean our conscience represents our soul, or is it a part of it and if so, what is the relationship? I have always believed if a man has no conscience, his soul is without spirit and, therefore, he is dead on the inside.

In order for repentance to occur, one must first be aware of and understand the sin committed and have a sense of guilt, regret or remorse. This is where my conscience plays an enormous role in true remorse and true repentance. We have all done something that we regret, are not proud of or are sorry for. But if we had to do it over, we still wouldn't have a change of heart. If we remain steadfast in our convictions, we may be blindsided by truth. Without compunction or an act of contrition, there is neither repentance nor forgiveness. So how do we wipe the slate clean? We don't. God does, and all we have to do is ask. *"I tell you that in the same way, there will be more joy in heaven over one sinner who repents than over ninety-nine righteous persons who need no repentance." Luke 15:7*

It was during my life and death struggle with cancer that I became aware of angels who watched over me, comforted and protected me along my physical journey. These angels also provide a spiritual communion with God and taught me how to receive divine guidance. I have learned that to judge is to protect...not the one you judge but yourself. When I adjudicate others, angels are quickly summoned to open my heart, mind and soul. Without covering, the self-righteous stand naked to invaders who can examine your inner self. The mirror image may be displeasing to the eye as you attempt to cover your transgressions.

Teacher, they do not walk with me as you do, my mentor and spiritual advisor, for they are hovering in a flutter above me. I am vaguely aware of their presence. I now believe everyone has guiding angels through life's journey. Have you seen yours or are you aware of their presence? Hold my hand, walk with me and be patient, for we have much to learn from one another.

Sincerely,

Your student, a disciple of Christ

Epilogue

Can cancer cure cancer? For most of my life I was infected with a materialistic cancer. It spread from my mind to my heart and ultimately my soul. I was not a bad or evil person, but money and my time was at the top of my prideful list of me, myself and I accomplishments. Then I was blessed with a real life-threatening cancer of the body. I did say blessed because I believe this cancer was a cure for my spiritual cancer and saved my immortal soul. Contrary to popular belief, you can take it with you…your soul, that is.

I have learned the true value of my precious time. To give it freely and share the Jesus-like qualities that are in all of us. The importance of others far outweighs self-importance. Lend a hand rather than turn a blind eye. Don't burden others with the weight of your own shortcomings. Listen to others rather than hammer them with your own thoughts, wishes and desires.

Before cancer my eyes were open, yet I did not see. I have learned the blind may see better than the gifted and even the deaf can hear the calling of Jesus.

If you managed to make it this far, my prayers are with you. Before I pray, I am aware that God sees my sins. When I begin to pray, I ask God for forgiveness first, so I can go about prayer uninhibited by the weight of sin. Looking through life's window, God observes His child stumble and fall. I pick myself up and run to my Father who listens, consoles and cleanses the wounds of sin through prayer.

Would you pray with me?

Come Holy Spirit! Heavenly Father, fill us with peace. Let us never forget the infinite possibilities that are born of faith. Sweet Jesus, let your presence settle into our bones and allow our souls the freedom to sing your praises, for you, Lord, are what miracles are made of. Father, we gladly share your love with our brothers and sisters, for when we look upon their faces, their eyes tell us that we will spend eternity with you in your glory.

My Lord, God and Father I trust in the blood of your Son Christ Jesus to cleanse me from sin. I believe Christ died for me and rose from the dead. I repent of my sins and will trust in Jesus to take me to be with you in heaven for He is the way, the truth, and the life. I accept you as my Lord and Savior in Jesus' name, amen.

Although I felt compelled to write this book, there were times I was tempted to give up, but I couldn't. I knew if it could bring comfort to just one heart or bring one soul to the Lord, it would be worth it. I leave you with this blessing. I pray that you will take a "leap" of faith and Fully Rely On God (**F.R.O.G.**).

"The LORD bless you, and keep you; The LORD make His face shine on you, And be gracious to you; The LORD lift up His countenance on you, And give you peace." Numbers 6:24–26